T0330550

Strategic Excellence in the Architecture, Engineering, and Construction Industries

Strategic Excellence in the Architecture, Engineering, and Construction Industries
How AEC Firms Can Develop and Execute Strategy Using Lean Six Sigma

Gerhard Plenert, PhD
Joshua Plenert, PE

Routledge
Taylor & Francis Group

A PRODUCTIVITY PRESS BOOK

Routledge
Taylor & Francis Group
711 Third Avenue, New York, NY 10017

International Standard Book Number-13: 978-1-138–47885-5 (Hardback)
International Standard Book Number-13: 978-1-351–04548-3 (eBook)

Visit the Taylor & Francis Web site at
www.taylorandfrancis.com

and the Productivity Press site at
www.ProductivityPress.com

To my beautiful wife for being my inspiration,

To my amazing kids for being my motivation,

And to my parents for their dedication.

Joshua Plenert

Contents

PHASE II Define: Establishing the Best Path to the Ideal Future State

PHASE III   Execute: Engaging
and Aligning the Organization

PHASE IV Refine: Stimulating Continuous Improvement through Cultural Vitality

Introduction

Most AEC (Architectural, Engineering, and Construction) firms seem to suffer from similar challenges. The workload seems to always be either a feast or a famine. The review process seems to be an obstacle and prevents staff members from meeting deadlines. The available resources seem to constantly be dedicated to firefighting, always overwhelmed by the most urgent tasks and never able to get to the most important tasks. Incentive programs seem to create silos throughout the organization resulting in a lack of organization-wide unity. New employees seem to quickly lose excitement for the job and end up leaving within a year. A lack of direction and passion has resulted in employees who seem to only do the bare minimum necessary to keep their jobs. Everyone is aware of the problems, everyone complains about the problems, but nothing ever changes. I'm sure you can add many more issues to the list.

The fact that these types of issues are so common among so many AEC firms should be exciting to you. Why? Because problems that are common among most AEC firms are great opportunities. The organization that can overcome common challenges will gain an uncommon competitive advantage. That is the purpose of this new book, *Strategic Excellence*. It helps you to develop a strategy for long-term sustainable excellence founded in a vibrant and productive culture of strategic thinking and continuous improvement.

When strategy and culture are efficaciously partnered, an organization can obtain a level of competitive advantage that cannot be copied by competitors. Tools, processes, even methods can be copied, but culture can never be copied. Strategic Excellence is a cultural approach that not only develops what your organization does, but what your organization is and what it is becoming. That's what makes Strategic Excellence effective. That's what makes it sustainable. That's what will render your competition irrelevant.

Authors

Joshua Plenert is a licensed professional engineer and is currently serving as a regional manager for an engineering and architectural firm where he has played a major role in the development of two branch offices. Joshua's educational background consists of a BS in civil engineering, an MS in structural engineering, and an MBA. He has worked in various aspects of the AEC industry for more than 14 years. His construction experience includes more than 8 years working in all phases of construction, construction management, facilities management, and project management. His engineering experience includes nearly 6 years of structural engineering, project management, engineering management, and business development. Joshua has also enjoyed teaching engineering courses as an adjunct professor.

Dr. Gerhard Plenert, former director of executive education at the Shingo Institute, has more than 25 years of professional experience in organizational transformations helping companies and government agencies strive for enterprise excellence by utilizing the Shingo Model to drive cultural transformations. Dr. Plenert is an internationally recognized expert in supply chain management; Lean/Six Sigma; IT; quality and productivity tools; and in working with leading-edge planning and scheduling methods. He has literally "written the book" on leading-edge supply chain management concepts, such as finite capacity scheduling, advanced planning and scheduling, and world-class management.

His experience includes significant initiatives with Genentech, Johnson & Johnson, Aerojet Rocketdyne, Shell, Aramco, Sony, Cisco, Microsoft, Seagate, NCR Corporation, Ritz-Carlton, the US Air Force, and numerous other branches of the US Department of Defense. Additionally, Dr. Plenert has served as a consultant to major manufacturing and distribution companies, such as Hewlett-Packard, Black & Decker, Raytheon, Motorola, Applied Magnetics, Toyota, AT&T, IBM, and Kraft Foods. He has also been considered a corporate "guru" on supply chain management for Wipro, AMS, and Infosys, and a Lean/Six Sigma "guru" for the US Air Force and various consulting companies.

With 14 years of academic experience, Dr. Plenert has published over 150 articles and 22 books on Lean, supply chain strategy, operations management and planning. He has written MBA textbooks and operations planning books for the United Nations. Dr. Plenert's ideas and publications have been endorsed by people like Stephen Covey and companies such as Motorola, AT&T, Black & Decker, and FedEx. His publications are viewable at www.gerhardplenert.com.

Dr. Plenert previously served as a tenured full professor at California State University, Chico; a professor at BYU, BYU–Hawaii, University of Malaysia, University of San Diego; and has been a visiting professor at numerous universities all over the world. He earned degrees in math, physics, and German; and he holds an MBA, MA in international studies, and PhD in resource economics (oil and gas) and operations management. Dr. Plenert continues to serve as a Shingo examiner and as an adjunct faculty member for several universities.

1

Strategic Excellence

1.1 INTRODUCTION

Strategic Excellence is a goal and a process. Excellence is a moving target. Like airbags in cars, what was considered above and beyond normal and a level of excellence 10 years ago is routine today. The goal of Strategic Excellence is a moving target and needs to be reviewed at least annually.

Strategic Excellence is also a process in that it requires a focus on continuous improvement. Strategic excellence is applied strategic thinking designed to develop an empowered agile strategy that adapts to changing circumstances and drives a high performing culture of striving towards ideal behaviors. It is infused with the insight and the thought leadership of the Shingo Model and the scientific thinking of Lean Six Sigma, as derived from the Toyota Production System (TPS). Strategic Excellence goes beyond the classic approach to strategic planning by driving effective execution of the strategy by embedding collective ownership and organization-wide alignment into the entire process.

Reflecting on TPS, Toyota Engineering's approach is extremely different from the American automakers, such as Ford or General Motors. When Toyota engineers a new automobile, it generally takes less than 6 months. When the American auto manufacturer engineers a new vehicle model, it generally takes over 3 years, although they are now trying to gradually improve the process. There are numerous examples of how this process is manifested. One quick example can be found in the airbag. The airbag was an invention by American automakers, but Toyota was the first to install airbags in their automobiles.

So, what's the difference between Toyota and General Motors or Ford? Toyota manufacturers focus on quality. For example, if they design a hinge for a car door, and they find that the hinge has high quality, high reliability, product consistency, etc., they will use that same hinge in all of their vehicles. In contrast, when American auto manufacturers design a new vehicle, they reengineer everything, right down to the door hinges. The result is twofold: (1) American engineers take a lot longer to engineer a car and (2) American cars have hundreds of times as many recalls as cars manufactured by Toyota. However, when Toyota has a recall, it's large because it affects a large number of vehicle models.

To compare Toyota and the American manufacturers, let's consider the effect of the different methodologies. Which is more customer responsive by having a higher level of product flexibility? Which methodology tends to have higher quality and reliability? What characteristics do you, the reader, prefer in the products that you purchase? Which of these two engineering strategies would you classify as having strategic excellence?

Strategic excellence is not an accident. It doesn't happen by chance. It requires intelligent planning and deliberate action. Strategic excellence is the prerequisite for achieving a corporate vision. It is the only path to victory.

On June 6, 1944, the Allied forces crashed onto the beaches of Normandy. The D-Day campaign involved more than 13,000 aircraft, 5,000 ships, and 150,000 troops from eight different Allied countries. The Allied forces had been working together for many months in preparation for that day by spreading out Nazi forces using a variety of tactics. Despite the unprecedented amount of coordination required to execute an operation of this size, when the smoke cleared, the Allied forces had established a solid foothold in Europe. This extraordinary victory was referred to by Winston Churchill as "the beginning of the end."

Dwight D. Eisenhower stated that "in preparing for battle I have always found that plans are useless, but planning is indispensable". When the Allied forces landed on the beaches, chaos ensued. Surely, many aspects of the invasion didn't go exactly as planned. However, the many months of planning had prepared the Allied forces to succeed, no matter what scenario they were challenged with when they hit the beach.

The message of this story is that it's the process of strategic planning, the analysis of the options, and the consideration of alternative scenarios which is invaluable. The resulting plan will invariably change because the environment and the assumptions change. For example, the weather changes, the people change, the financial structure changes, the legal structure and the code structure change, and so on. The better you have thought through the various potential scenarios, the better prepared you are for the unexpected.

This book takes the "planning is indispensable" approach to strategic excellence. The planning process presented here will unite an organization behind a shared mission that will guide and direct decision making and problem solving at all levels. It will develop a culture that will prepare your organization to succeed, despite the scenario encountered.

1.2 PHASES

This book explores the Strategic Planning and Strategic Management processes by categorizing them into four functional phases. Strategic Planning is divided into two phases, which are thoroughly *analyze* the current and future conditions and then *define* a competitive strategic plan based on the analysis. These first two phases that we are grouping together as Strategic Planning are also often referred to as SA&D (Strategic Analysis and Design).

The second two phases are lumped together under the heading of Strategic Management. These phases are to *execute* the plan in an effective manner that will align the entire organization focused on the plan and then *refine* the plan over time, learning from our experiences to maintain a focus on continuous improvement (Chart 1.1).

1.2.1 Analyze

A successful planning process is built on a foundation involving a thorough understanding of current conditions. Far too often, engineering

CHART 1.1
Strategic Excellence Model.

becomes an exercise in what is referred to as Catalog Engineering. For example, Catalog Engineering frequently occurs when companies lay out their assembly lines. They search the catalogs put out by industrial machinery makers and they create some combination of different machines using machines that already exist, trying their best to make them work together successfully. Often, the job of making the pieces work together becomes someone else's problem, like production.

At Toyota, the engineer's job is not completed until he or she incorporates creativity into the newly created line. His or her job is to make the line better than the sum of its parts. The Analyze Phase defines the end product to be high quality and error-free. The engineer's job isn't finished until after the trial runs are completed and the assembly line is in full production, running with high quality and error-free. An example of how this works is that the production line must be sensitive enough to failures so that it stops itself automatically. No bad product should ever be produced. The Analyze Phase includes the requirement that the engineer must stay with the assembly line and continue refining the line until he/she achieves the goal of being error- and defect-free.

The Analyze Phase of this book explains the elements of both an internal analysis and an external analysis. Useful tools for ensuring a thorough analysis are presented and their usage is explained. The analysis process works to break through the cultural façade and identify the underlying issues that are typically overlooked. It forces the organization to ask the hard questions that many organizations subconsciously avoid asking themselves. Starting with a detailed analysis of the current state of the organization and the environment in which it operates and recognizing the gaps between the current state and the desired state will lead the organization towards developing a highly competitive strategy.

1.2.2 Define

Defining a strategic plan is often simplified by downloading a free template or slightly altering a previously used plan. This approach not only results in an uncustomized strategic plan but also completely misses out on the true power of strategic planning, which is the planning process itself. The methodology presented in this book will result in a highly competitive plan, customized for the specific strengths and needs of the organization. Additionally, it creates organizational buy-in. This means that the defined strategy is not only important to one person who tries in vain to execute it, but it becomes a shared vision that stimulates a sense of strategy ownership infused throughout the entire organization. The process of defining the strategy presented in this book will result in a plan that is primed to be successfully executed.

In the authors' experience as a consultant for organizations that have achieved enterprise excellence, it is common to walk around an organization and randomly ask employees what the goal/vision/mission is of the organization they work for. In most companies, it is rare to find someone who is even willing to attempt to guess what the company's vision is. But in Enterprise Excellent organizations, the employees know their organization's goals and they incorporate them into their daily activities, ensuring that what they do has strategic alignment. Try it in your organization. Randomly ask employees what the corporate vision is and see what you learn from their responses.

1.2.3 Execute

Executing a strategic plan can often be a frustrating endeavor, similar to initiating the movement of a heavy stationary object. The resting object tends to remain at rest. Tradition and a feeling of "we've always done it that way" tend to dominate and resist change. Getting a strategic plan to the point where it begins to build momentum and continues moving in the right direction can take significant time and energy. The Execute process presented in this book builds on the momentum created during the Define phase. When the entire organization is aligned with the strategy and buy-in has been established, executing the plan becomes the natural next step because every member of the organization is working to move the strategy in the right direction. The Execute phase presented in this book takes advantage of this momentum by strengthening the organizational alignment with the strategy, building engagement, and establishing effective visual management. This phase works to employ the strategy in such a way that it will act as a guide to decision making and problem solving at all levels of the organization. This process allows managers and staff to overcome challenges in ways that will support the vision/mission/goals of the organization and keep the momentum going.

1.2.4 Refine

An effective strategy cannot be stagnant. It is a living entity with the ability to learn and change. The Refine phase causes an evolutionary adjustment to the strategic plan, giving it the inherent ability to analyze and respond to internal and external changes. It creates a culture of learning that perceives problems as opportunities and facilitates an organization-wide philosophy of continuous improvement. It establishes a continual loop of learning and improving that will propel your organization to the front of the pack and keep it there. The Refine phase presented in this book keeps the organization current and competitive.

At Mitsubishi, an experiment was conducted called a "Purpose Expansion." Employees tracked all of their activities for a 2-week period. They recorded what they did and how much time they spent doing it. This exercise had to be prefaced with a corporate commitment that no employees would lose their jobs. After 2 weeks, the employees summarized their activities using a spreadsheet. In the second column of the spreadsheet, they were asked to indicate the purpose of each activity. In the third column of the spreadsheet, they were asked to indicate the purpose of the items listed in the second column of the spreadsheet. In the fourth column of the spreadsheet, they had to indicate if the purpose that they listed in the third column satisfied the vision/mission of the organization, which was to either (1) increase customer satisfaction or (2) increase quality. These two items were, of course, the strategic objectives of Mitsubishi. The fourth column allowed for three responses: (1) Yes, the purpose satisfied one of the strategic objectives, or (2) No, the purpose had no effect or possibly even detracted from the strategic objective, or (3) the employee wasn't sure if the activity was supportive on or not. If the activity listed in the first column had a "NO" response in the fourth column, then the employee was to immediately cease doing that activity. The result was an almost exact one-third split between each of the three responses, which meant that one-third of the activities of the employees was stopped. These activities were considered to be a "waste" since they did not improve on the organization's goals. This new free time was then allocated to spending more time on the one-third of the activities that had a "YES" response. Mitsubishi was able to refine and improve their process using this simple Purpose Expansion exercise. (For a detailed discussion of this experiment, refer to the book, *Making Innovation Happen: Concept Management through Integration*, Delray Beach, Florida, St. Lucie Press, by Gerhard Plenert and Shozo Hibino.)

1.3 SUMMARY

The authors have lost count of the number of times they have conducted an Enterprise Excellence seminar in a company and asked the attendees to write down the company's vision or mission statements. The employees walk by the statements every day as they enter the building. They may even have been involved in the creation of these statements. But they don't remember what they are. So, the next question that must be asked is, "Are the activities that you are doing daily, or is the job that you are doing, achieving the vision of the company if you don't even know what it is?"

Significant advances in strategic planning and management have been developed over decades of learning and practice. However, many of those advances have been developed in the manufacturing industry and have not been translated into terms easily applicable to the AEC (Architectural, Engineering, and Construction) industry. This book incorporates the current best practices from cutting-edge organizations around the globe and presents those practices in a way that they can be applied easily, efficiently, and effectively to AEC organizations. This book applies proven Shingo and TPS Lean Six Sigma methods and tools to the strategic planning and management processes in a uniquely new methodology that the AEC industry has never seen.

The approach of this book is not just to develop a strategic plan, but to develop a strategic way a thinking. It's a cultural approach to creating and maintaining a competitive edge. It challenges the status quo in order to advance beyond it. Shigeo Shingo said, "those who are not dissatisfied will never make any progress". Strategic Excellence in the AEC industry will allow you and your organization to drastically reverse long-endured dissatisfaction and a lack of progress into exceptional forward surges.

Phase I

Analyze: Diving Deep into Current Conditions

2

Introduction to Analysis

2.1 INTRODUCTION

When Dr. Gerhard Plenert was traveling in Japan working with his co-author on a different book, he would often join in with a group of academics and Toyota executives to discuss Toyota Production System principles. One night, during one of these discussions, the conversation turned to the United States. One executive asked, "Do you want to know what's wrong with the United States?" Unfortunately, this is a conversation that occurs far too often during international travels. Everyone seems to know what's wrong with the United States and they are eager to share their insights on how to fix the issues.

Dr. Plenert was tempted to answer by saying, "No. But I can tell you what's wrong with Japan." Instead, he answered, "Tell me what you think is wrong with the U.S."

The executive came back with a very Lean answer. He suggested, "You're creating far too much non-value-added content."

Dr. Plenert responded, "What does that mean?"

The executive drew a diagram on a piece of paper (see Chart 2.1) as he said, "Look at the students that you are graduating from your universities. You're graduating an ever-increasing number of non-value-added students and an ever-decreasing number of value-added students. The non-value-added students are using up resources, or at best just moving them around. But the overall value of the nation is not increasing in proportion to the size of the population. The United States isn't producing enough resources to sustain its current standard of living in the long run."

All Dr. Plenert could say was, "That's a very interesting perspective."

The executive ended with the comment, "You need to shift the culture in the United States to be more focused on creating value. You need to

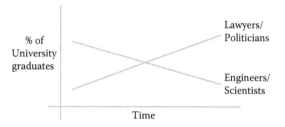

CHART 2.1
Decrease in value-adding graduates.

change the way people think so that your students will want to enter into professions that grow the country, rather than just burn up its valuable content."

Dr. Plenert responded by smiling and saying, "I'll hurry back and tell our president what he needs to do to fix America."

"Excellent," was the executive's response.

The purpose of this story is to make you, the reader, think. Are we creating value as a nation? As a government (federal, state, local)? As a company or agency? What do you, the reader, think? What about our culture? Is it based on principles? Is there a set of principles, like the Shingo Principles, that should be considered for the nation as a whole? The point we are trying to make here is that all organizations at all levels from the nation as a whole, down to the family or even the individual, need to take a "big picture" look at what they are doing. Do we have goals and objectives? Are they based on principles that we believe in and live by? Do we have a strategy for meeting those goals? These are important thoughts that you need to consider, but for now, we need to have a starting point, and that starting point is you and your company. How can we make your enterprise excellent?

Most of us are familiar with the saying "garbage in, garbage out". The saying is just as true in strategic planning as it is in engineering calculations. The Analyze Phase of strategic planning is the input and strategic excellence is the desired output. If you expect your strategic planning process to result in a highly competitive strategy, then you must take the time to conduct a thorough analysis of current conditions. Likewise, if you expect the planning process to prepare the organization to face changing conditions, you must take the time to consider multiple potential future scenarios to prevent being caught off guard when they arise. A garbage analysis will surely result in a garbage strategy.

It's fairly obvious that one of the primary purposes of the Analyze Phase is to develop an understanding of the current and potential future conditions that will be used to develop a winning strategy. However, the Analyze Phase presented in this book has a hidden agenda, that is, to tear down the organization's façade that has been set so solidly over years of complacency. Most organizations tend to find their "comfort zone" and then continue to operate within that zone for years, sometimes decades, without ever asking themselves if there's a better way. In fact, I'm sure every professional in the AEC industry has heard on numerous occasions the saying "we don't need to reinvent the wheel." This attitude results from a fear of change that prevents many organizations from ever reaching a highly competitive status in a modern environment. Maintaining a competitive edge requires continuous improvement, which means that your organization must regularly reevaluate its strategic position. If you're not advancing, you're not keeping up. If you're not moving forward, then everyone else will pass you by and you'll soon find yourself falling behind.

2.2 WHY ANALYZE?

It is common for the leadership of AEC firms to be tempted to skip the analysis phase and jump right into development of the strategy. This temptation must be avoided. A thorough analysis is a critical step in the strategic planning process. Developing a strategy without performing an analysis is similar to designing a building without first determining the applied loads in order to size the columns, beams, connections, etc. The result may be a beautifully detailed building that is not suited to withstand the necessary loading conditions. The structural elements meant to keep the building standing will likely fail when they're needed the most. Likewise, skipping the Analyze Phase in the strategic planning process may result in a well-organized strategy that looks great on paper but cannot effectively be executed because it is not well suited for the current environment and will likely fail when stress occurs to the system and when it's needed the most.

The prominent organizational theorist and author of *The Mind of the Strategist* said that "analysis is the critical starting point of strategic thinking." To conduct a serious analysis, it is helpful to understand the value of the analysis. Let's discuss a few of the major benefits of a thorough analysis.

2.2.1 Problems = Opportunities

Analyzing your organization will undoubtedly bring to light many issues that the organization has spent years avoiding. Admitting to yourself that the organization you've dedicated so much time to may not be as flawless as you've convinced yourself can be a painful realization. In fact, the desire to avoid dealing with the problems can subconsciously prevent us from seeing the problems in the first place. The analysis process presented in this book will help you and your organization to overcome the fear of facing your problems by redefining them as opportunities. Lee Iacocca said, "We are continually faced with great opportunities brilliantly disguised as insoluble problems."

Another way of thinking about this concept is to recognize that most of the problems your organization is facing most likely exist within your competitor's organizations as well. This suggests that if you are able to overcome these problems, you will win a competitive advantage. Thus, every problem identified in the Analyze Phase of the strategic planning process is literally an opportunity to improve your organization and move into a more competitive position. Failing to solve the problem or even failing to recognize the problem in the first place is a missed opportunity. Every innovation begins with recognizing a problem and having the foresight and wisdom to interpret it as an opportunity.

Viewing every problem as an opportunity will facilitate a more thorough and informative analysis. It is by identifying and understanding the problems that effective solutions can be developed. Although the problems may seem to be many, an effective strategy with only a few properly developed objectives can often resolve many problems. Don't fear the problems, seek them out like gold.

2.2.2 One Size Does Not Fit All

Far too often, managers will attempt to advance their own organizations by copying what other organizations are doing. The problem with this approach is twofold. First, if you are trying to compete with other organizations by copying their strategy, then you will never be able to accomplish anything more than just catching up. Second, when it comes to strategic plans, one size does not fit all. A strategy that works miracles for one firm may be ineffective or even destructive to another. Variations in cultures, markets, and clients can demand very different strategies.

A competitive strategy is one that is customized for the specific needs of your organization.

The analysis process will dive deep into the organization from multiple perspectives and work to pull out the root causes of the problems. It will focus on gaining a detailed understanding of what the organization is capable of and what challenges and opportunities it faces. The analysis will also develop an understanding of a number of potential future scenarios that your organization may be required to face. By understanding the organization in such an intimate way, you will be able to develop a strategic plan that is highly customized for your specific needs. Additionally, as the plan is executed, this deep understanding of your organization will prepare you to adapt to changing conditions as needed. Every highly competitive strategy is customized to make the organization stand out, not make it blend in.

2.2.3 Reinvent the Wheel

The invention of the wheel was no doubt an impressive innovation. However, it is the countless times the wheel has been reinvented that has driven the transportation industry to where it's at today. Without the reinvention of the wheel, we would still be stuck trying to use the original design. It's alarming how many managers have stubbornly adhered to the "don't reinvent the wheel" mindset. Why would you not want to reinvent the wheel? Is your goal to reduce cost, or to achieve Strategic Excellence? Do you want to remain in your current state forever, never growing and never differentiating yourself as an excellent competitor? If so, then, "don't reinvent the wheel."

The Analyze Phase is designed to shake things up. It's designed to force your organization to ask the hard questions. It drives a new way of thinking. It highlights the flaws in the wheel so that it can be reinvented. In other words, it creates an opportunity for your organization to ask, "Is the way we've always done this really the best way of doing it?" and "How can we improve our approach and gain a more competitive edge?"

Strategic excellence isn't about being complacent with your comfort zone. It's about developing strategic thinking in order to drive innovation. It's about identifying and then bridging the gap between where you are and where you would like to be. In most cases, it's not about who came up with the wheel, it's about who has the best wheel or who has a unique wheel. In the AEC industry, it's not about who invented architecture, it's about which organization provides the best architectural services. Achieving Strategic Excellence in the AEC industry is all about reinventing the wheel.

2.3 ANALYSIS APPROACH

The analysis approach presented in this book focuses on developing understanding. That is, it treats the process of pursuing understanding as the most valuable aspect of the analysis. Many of the obvious challenges that organizations are faced with are actually symptoms of underlying problems. Taking the time to develop an intimate understanding of your organization will allow you to focus on curing the concealed root causes of the problems rather than just relieving the more noticeable symptoms. Long-lasting relief of symptoms will occur once the underlying problems have been addressed.

An intimate understanding of your organization is achieved by approaching the analysis from multiple perspectives. First, potential future scenarios are considered in detail including best-case, worst-case, and most-likely scenarios. Each scenario is analyzed to assess several potential impacts on the organization, such as financial impacts, cultural impacts, and operational impacts. Second, the organization is analyzed from an internal perspective. The internal analysis will include examining various internal aspects, such as culture, operations, and core competencies. Finally, the organization is analyzed from an external perspective. An external analysis considers environmental impacts, economic changes, potential opportunities, and client relationships (Chart 2.2).

The analysis will also require the input of several key individuals from within and outside the organization. One person alone cannot see the

CHART 2.2
Strategic Excellence Model – Analyze Phase.

organization from sufficient perspectives to develop a full "high-level" understanding. Obtaining more perspectives will provide valuable insight and will work to break through individual biases.

2.4 SUMMARY

The analysis is the foundation on which is built the entire strategy. Investing time and resources into the analysis will pay significant dividends in the long run. However, as you conduct your analysis, it is essential to keep in mind the purpose of the analysis. The purpose is to gain sufficient understanding of underlying problems and the missed opportunities so that they can be resolved. Don't focus on the problems any more than necessary to be prepared to develop a solution. Engineers, architects, and other analytical thinkers have developed a keen ability to identify problems. Often, the problems that are the focus of your attention are symptoms of a larger, "higher-level" systemic issue and solving the specific problem only results in moving the problem to a different system. For example, if there is a quality problem where the measurements are not within the required specifications, the solution tends to be to introduce a control point or an inspection point that attempts to verify the measurement. However, introducing another control point has a negative effect on the overall system. An additional control point will (1) increase the complexity of the process, (2) make the process take longer, and (3) introduce another failure point. Instead, we should examine the source of the metric failure to identify how we can improve the quality.

Too often, engineers focus all of their energy on simply identifying all the problems and they have little attention span left to dedicate to solving the problems. Your analysis should always be conducted with the purpose of the analysis in mind. Heed the advice of Alan Scharf in the book "Breakthrough Thinking": "Don't become an expert about the problem" (Nadler and Hibino, 1994). Instead, become an expert in developing high-level systemic solutions.

Nadler and Hibino provide additional insight with the following explanation:

> The indiscriminate amassing of information inherent in "finding out all there is to know" not only wastes time, effort, and money, it can

actually impede solution of a problem by burying you under an avalanche of irrelevant, unmanageable detail. In short, it causes, "analysis-paralysis."

Nadler and Hibino, 1994

In the United States, the tendency is to first collect data and then use the data to identify the problem. Toyota condemns this approach as a waste of time in that we spend months collecting data and then come to conclusions that focus too much on symptoms. Their approach is to first do a purpose expansion to find out if the problem is worth solving, making sure that solving the problem is relevant for achieving the goals of the organization. Then, the next step is to find the "high-level" system within which the failure is occurring. This is followed by studying the system and the behaviors that it triggers, which may or may not involve data collection. But the key message here is that data, in and of itself, is not always a good thing as data seem to be the general attitude of the American industry.

Take the analysis process seriously but keep in mind that the purpose of the analysis is to develop solutions, not to amass huge amounts of data. The analysis process presented in this book will help you and your organization to focus your efforts to avoid wasting time on collecting data and analyzing information that will not contribute to the solution. It will help you gain an intimate and results-oriented understanding through concentrated scrutiny rather than a broad accumulation of information.

3

Visioning and Scenario Planning

3.1 INTRODUCTION

Visioning and scenario planning are a critical part of the United States military strategic planning effort. As noted at the start of the first chapter, the planning process forces the military to look at alternatives before a situation occurs and allows them to be prepared and be at the leading edge. Similarly, major successful enterprises, like Toyota, spend a large amount of time in visioning exercises. That was how they were able to successfully take over as the leader in the international automotive industry. When Toyota took the lead in automotive sales, *The New York Times* had a headline indicating that GM had lost its position as the world leader. The following day, GM gave their response, which was that they aren't bothered that Toyota sold more cars, GM was still the leader in that they built more cars. So, what is the goal? To build more cars or to sell more cars? What is the vision of these two auto makers? And who needed a Federal Government bailout?

Visioning and scenario planning is the process of looking into the future and attempting to plan for a variety of possible future scenarios. It allows a firm to be more prepared when things don't go the way you were expecting them to. A great definition of can be found in the book, *Scenario Planning in Organizations*, written by Thomas Chermack:

> Performance-based scenario planning is a discipline of building a set of internally consistent and imagined futures in which decisions about the future can be played out, for the purpose of changing thinking, improving decision making, fostering human and organization learning and improving performance.
>
> **Chermack, 2011**

In the United States, we tend to follow the Dr. Phil philosophy: "The best predictor of future behavior is past behavior." That may be true when analyzing individual behavior, but that is not true in running a business. For example, following the traditional approach, if we are a manufacturer of toilets, then we would look to the past and see how many toilets we sold in the last few years and use that measure to predict how many toilets we plan to sell next year. This approach is referred to as focusing on lagging indicators to predict future events. An alternative approach, which uses leading indicators as the predictor, is to focus on housing starts and use that number to predict future toilet sales. Leading indicators tend to be more accurate and more reliable, but they are not as easy to access, and we, therefore, default to the easier lagging indicator numbers. Similarly, visioning and scenario planning apply the use of leading indicators to prepare us for future events. They take more work, but they are significantly more accurate.

Visioning and scenario planning is more than a simple prediction of what is most likely to happen; it also considers other potential scenarios, even if they don't seem to be very likely to occur. It is by considering even the unlikely scenarios at each end of the realm of possibilities that we can be better prepared for any scenario that lies in-between. It would be a serious mistake to assume that things will continue as they are now. The reality is that the world and the AEC industry are constantly changing. The process can be difficult for scientific minds because we are used to applying math and physics to arrive at THE answer. However, in scenario planning, THE one correct answer doesn't exist. Indeed, we can say that the Schrödinger's Cat thought experiment applies. Every potential scenario can be thought of as reality until the box is actually opened. Organizations will not always be able to predict what is going to happen 10 years from now and they often cannot even successfully predict what will happen 1 year from now. Visioning and scenario planning will help you and your organization to better prepare for the unexpected changes that will inevitably occur.

3.2 PERSPECTIVES

Visioning and scenario planning will work to apply various perspectives in order to gain a more complete picture of what the future may look like. These perspectives are analyzed at several points along a time line. The time line should be extended well into the future and should be considered a long-range visioning exercise. The points along the time line that are most often analyzed are 5, 10, and 20 years into the future. Many organizations will resist looking too far into the future and will stick to a short-range visioning exercise. Short-range visioning exercises are far less effective because they will focus more on simply maintaining the organization rather than inspiring innovation and driving the organization towards long-term success. Many of the most important improvements that an organization can make will take years to fully realize. A short-range visioning exercise will result in temporary relief of symptoms rather than in long-term solutions. Some of the most innovative and successful organizations in the world, which include several Japanese firms, perform visioning exercises that extend 100 years and beyond.

The perspectives that must be considered at each time interval are political, economic, social, technological, legal, and environmental (PESTLE).

The **Political** perspective considers the impact that potential political decisions can have on your organization. These impacts may include changes to labor laws, trade restrictions, political instability, changes to healthcare policies, changes to immigration policies, changes to the education system, fluctuations in infrastructure funding, etc.

The **Economic** perspective evaluates potential economic changes that can impact your organization. These may include fluctuations in the national and global economies, changes in tax requirements, rising and falling interest rates, changes in the cost of living, changes in the cost of operating a business, etc.

The **Social** perspective considers changes that may occur in the society in which the organization is operating. These changes may include population increases and decreases in geographical areas, cultural diversity within the workforce, changing social views that may increase the customers' expectations, etc.

The **Technological** perspective considers changes that may occur in the tech industry that can impact your organization in either positive or negative ways. Some examples may include advances in analysis and design software, the increasing impact of social media, the ever-advancing communication applications, the increasing ability to employ a remote workforce, etc.

The **Legal** perspective evaluates potential changes in legal systems that can affect your organization and how it does business. The legal perspective may consider changes to employment laws, increasing requirements in health and safety laws, changes in consumer laws, etc.

The **Environmental** perspective considers the impact that environmental forces can have on your organization. Some environmental considerations may include storm activity and other natural disasters, limited geographical space, diminishing reserves of natural resources, etc.

3.3 VISIONING AND SCENARIO PLANNING PROCEDURE

The recommended procedure for executing visioning and scenario planning comes from the book, *Driving Strategy to Execution Using Lean Six Sigma*, written by Gerhard Plenert and Tom Cluley (2012). This procedure follows these five steps:

1. Leadership Orientation
2. Orientation Briefing
3. Visioning Assignment
4. Visioning Workshop
5. Post-workshop Wrap-Up

3.3.1 Step 1 – Leadership Orientation

The leadership orientation involves meeting with the top three or four individuals in the organization to explain the visioning and scenario planning process. The organization's leaders need to be on board with the process to prevent leadership questioning while the process is being conducted. The leadership orientation is meant to help create unity within the leadership of the organization to gain their support of the process. It is also an opportunity to discuss what the leadership team hopes to get out of the process. Understanding their expectations may impact the way the visioning and scenario planning process is conducted. For example, the leadership team may want the exercise carried out for a 100-year time line instead of a 20-year time line. The leadership orientation should result in a united effort to achieve common outcomes.

3.3.2 Step 2 – Orientation Briefing

The orientation briefing is a short introduction of the visioning and scenario planning process to all those who will be participating in the exercise.

The visioning facilitator should explain the importance of the visioning exercise and emphasize the necessity for all to participate in the process. Participation will provide more insightful outcomes. Then, the facilitator should explain each of the PESTLE perspectives in terms that apply to your specific organization and introduce the visioning assignment.

3.3.3 Step 3 – Visioning Assignment

The visioning assignment requires that each participant in the visioning workshop analyze the organization based on two of the PESTLE perspectives at 5, 10, and 20 years and ensures that the assignments are evenly spread so that each perspective is thoroughly analyzed. Each participant needs to identify the major trends for his/her assigned perspectives at each time period and write them down on sticky notes. The participants should be given at least a week to complete their investigations. The investigations should include discussions with other people both inside and outside the organization. Research should include reading articles, analyzing competitors, searching reliable sources online, and reaching out to other professionals. The participants should bring to the visioning workshop all of their sticky notes with their 5-, 10-, and 20-year trends.

3.3.4 Step 4 – Visioning Workshop

The visioning workshop reviews each of the PESTLE perspectives one at a time, commencing with the 5-year time line and discussing potential trends at each of the six perspectives. The discussion should be led by the facilitator but the participants should be the ones to explain the trends they have identified during their research. As the participants discuss the trends for the 5-year time line, the sticky notes should be posted on a whiteboard. Before the sticky notes are posted, the facilitator draws a horizontal access at the bottom of the board and titles it "Impact," with the low end indicated at the left and the high end indicated at the right (Chart 3.1). The sticky notes should then be posted along the line based on relative impact. The following figure illustrates an example of trends on a whiteboard based on relative impact.

Once all of the sticky notes are posted along the horizontal access, the discussion should shift away from impact and turn towards uncertainty. The facilitator draws a vertical axis on the left side of the whiteboard and title it "Uncertainty," with the low end noted at the bottom and the high

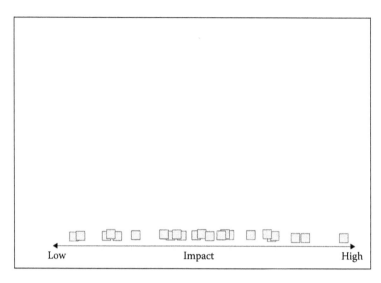

CHART 3.1
Impact of trends.

end noted at the top. Then, each trend should be discussed and the sticky notes should be moved up the board based on their level of uncertainty. The following figure illustrates an example of the completed Impact-Uncertainty Matrix (Chart 3.2).

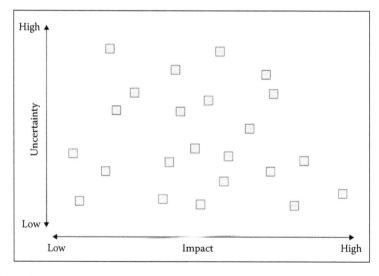

CHART 3.2
Impact vs. Uncertainty of trends.

This process should then be repeated for the 10-year and 20-year time frame. Once all three Impact-Uncertainty matrices have been developed, the group should move to a discussion on scenarios. For each of the three time frames, the participants should discuss what the best-case scenario, the worst-case scenario, and most-likely case scenarios would be. These three scenarios are a minimum, but other scenarios should also be considered, especially if they have an equal likelihood of occurring. The participants should discuss how prepared the organization is to face each scenario and what the organization can do to better prepare for each scenario.

The key points of each of the three scenarios should be listed on a whiteboard, emphasizing the key influential trends that were taken from the Impact-Uncertainty Matrix. Also, the participants should list the effect and influence that each of the scenarios has on the enterprise, and how the enterprise might need to respond to each of the scenarios.

3.3.5 Step 5 – Post-workshop Wrap-Up

The three Impact-Uncertainty matrices should be recorded in a summarizing report along with any valuable insights that emerged during the visioning workshop. The report should also record the best-case, worst-case, and most-likely case scenarios for all three time frames, along with the organization's preparedness for each scenario and what the organization can do to better prepare. This report will then be used during the Analyze Phase, as discussed in the following chapters. The visioning and scenario planning process should be repeated once per year and the report from the previous year should be reviewed as part of the process to ensure that no key points are missed.

3.4 SUMMARY

Effective visioning and scenario planning can work to prevent creating a strategy that moves the organization in the wrong direction. It can prevent trying to change the direction of the organization after the proper momentum has already been developed. By preparing for a variety of potential scenarios, you and your organization can be prepared to succeed even in the worst-case scenario.

4

Internal Analysis

4.1 INTRODUCTION

An internal analysis is an examination of your organization's current operations, organizational structure, performance, and cultural well-being. It's an inward-looking audit of the organization with a focus on organizational health. Performing an internal analysis can provide valuable insight into the relationship between the organization and the employees. Developing an understanding of the current conditions associated with organizational life will result in an increase in social awareness allowing for a strategy that will enhance the lives of the employees and will simultaneously improve the bottom line of the company.

This chapter will present multiple considerations of an internal analysis and explain the importance of these considerations. Starting the strategy development process with an internal analysis will help your overall analysis identify the underlying problems rather than merely focus on the external symptoms. This approach will highlight why issues are occurring rather than just focus on what the issues are. This is the ultimate purpose of the analysis – to understand the root causes of problems so they can be resolved from the inside out. Understanding what is influencing negative behaviors will allow those influences to be corrected within the system, thus resulting in improved behaviors.

4.2 STRATEGY ANALYSIS

It is critical to start the analysis by evaluating the current corporate strategy. In some cases, it may take some digging to find it and in other cases, there may not actually be a strategy at all. Even if the organization just has a generic mission, start with what has already been created. There may be individuals within the organization who have been dedicating time, energy, and emotion to the development of the existing strategy. So, if the existing strategy is simply ignored or thrown out, it may result in frustration from those who have been developing and applying it. We need to build on the positive aspects of what has been developed, rather than just tear it down.

At the same time, if a strategy already exists, use it as a starting point but don't pass up the opportunity to enhance it. Look for any obvious shortcomings and highlight any strengths of the current strategy. Initially, the shortcomings may not be obvious. However, as you work your way through this book, the shortcomings will become more apparent. Evaluate whether the current plan appears to be appropriate for the current needs and challenges of the organization. Also, assess the effectiveness of how the current plan is being communicated and executed. Ask around and see how many employees know about the strategy and whether they feel motivated to support it.

The strategic plan should consist of a mission statement that clearly defines the purpose of the organization as well as a vision statement that outlines the firm's primary objectives for the future. The plan should also consist of well-defined values or principles as well as measurable strategic objectives. Employees at all levels of the organization must be actively engaged in supporting the strategy and must know what successful execution of the strategy looks like. If the employees at all levels of the organization do not clearly understand how their activities are supporting the strategic plan, then the current execution of the plan is not only ineffective but may turn out to be destructive.

Consider the case where the current strategic plan clearly defines what success looks like and how to achieve it. Consider the following example. The owner of an engineering firm visits a branch office and asks the employees if they are producing high-quality submittals. The employees struggle to provide an answer. The owner then proceeds to give a thorough explanation of why it's important to produce high-quality submittals. During the owner's next visit, he asks the employees if they are now producing high-quality submittals. Again, the employees struggle to answer the question, resulting in the owner feeling frustrated with the lack of attention to quality. The issue is not that the employees don't care about quality, the issue is that the employees don't have a clear and consistent view of what quality looks like. They don't know if the owner would consider what they are currently producing to be high quality or not. They also don't know what to change in order to achieve the owner's view of quality. A strategy that does not clearly define what success looks like and how to achieve it is not an executable strategy.

4.3 CULTURAL ANALYSIS

One of the major challenges facing every professional organization is attracting and retaining top talent. The organization's culture plays a major role in how long employees will stick around. Unfortunately, many organizations expect their organization's culture to magically develop into something great without any effort. The reality is that the organization's culture will develop on its own, but it is highly unlikely to become a healthy and productive culture if it is not effectively steered in that direction. Leaving the culture to manage itself is likely to have a detrimental effect on the organization. Even a fantastic strategy that is not designed to enhance the culture of the organization is unlikely to be successful. Culture is the lifeblood of the organization and will affect every one of the organization's undertakings. A positive and empowering culture will result in staff members performing at their best, even without their manager looking over their shoulder. Douglas Conant of Conant Leadership and former CEO of Campbell's Soup said, "to win in the marketplace you must first win in the workplace." This is why making organizational culture a priority is so critical. It will do more for your organization than every other leadership endeavor.

A cultural analysis is an evaluation of the current health of the organization's culture as well as an evaluation of how well the organization is managing the culture and moving it in the right direction. An analysis can typically be performed through interviews and surveys designed to obtain an understating of the organization's culture from multiple perspectives, such as the executive perspective, team leader perspective, staff perspective, and client perspective. Determine if a consistent culture exists and what the positive and negative aspects of the culture are. Do leaders dictate and micromanage or do they empower and mentor? Are employees engaged and do they have a positive outlook, or have they become passive and uninterested in improvement?

Is a positive culture being actively fostered? Consider the following example. The owner of an engineering firm discusses the importance of positive culture at every quarterly meeting. He explains that he wants employees to feel valued. Is it enough to simply give a speech at each quarterly meeting? Will that build a positive culture? If you are told every few months that you are supposed to feel valued, will that make you feel valued? Of course not. A positive culture is not built on good intentions; it is built on actions that reinforce the desired culture.

Far too many leaders consider "culture" to be a dirty word in that they do not have a clear grasp on what it means or how to influence it. Culture needs to be based on a set of principles which not only the leaders believe in but, through their example, the employees come to believe in. This belief in principles manifests itself in behaviors. If a leader walks into his or her organization and the employees give a quick brush off "hello" and then go back to what they were doing, this is a quick indicator that the employees aren't excited to see the leader. If you ask the employees a question, and they try to get rid of you quickly with a yes or no answer, that's not a good sign. But, if you ask the average employee what they're working on and they are excited to tell you and even go into more detail than you care to hear, then the culture is probably on the right track. A more complete discussion of culture and the influences on culture will be found in a subsequent chapter on the Shingo Principles.

One direct way to influence culture within an organization is through metrics. Management and corporate leaders need to learn that employees can make any measure look good. They're masters at making numbers look good, especially because they believe you're watching them. The trick is in the way the metrics are selected. If you select metrics that promote the type of behaviors that you want to see within the organization, then you will see a shift towards the type of culture you would like to see within the organization. Remember: One of the basic rules is that "too many metrics are as good as no metrics" because the employees don't know what target to shoot for. Select metrics that are simple and focused, and you'll get the desired results and build a successful culture. To get a detailed discussion on the importance of culture and its relationship to behaviors, look at the book, *Discover Excellence: An Overview of the Shingo Model and Its Principles (The Shingo Model Series)*.

4.4 OPERATIONS ANALYSIS

Operations analysis is a breakdown of the organization's operational systems in order to identify potential opportunities for improvement.

An operations analysis can become complex and can involve linear and nonlinear programming, network analyses, queuing systems, modeling, simulations, and more. However, in this book, we are focusing on developing strategic thinking and we won't be diving into the more complex aspects of operations analytics and optimization. Instead, we will focus on identifying the general aspects of the organizations' operations that may require additional action items. The operations analysis focuses on the following areas:

- Production Efficiency
- Quality
- Cost
- Value Stream
- Financial Performance
- Commercial Performance
- Continuous Improvement

4.4.1 Production Efficiency

The production efficiency of an organization's operations refers to how well the organization can get things done without wasting time, resources, and effort. It involves a careful comparison of production capacity and production demand to determine whether staff are being underutilized or overworked. Additionally, it requires consideration of how well the organization can respond to the client's demands. Are the organization's operations agile enough to be able to perform efficiently under varying conditions and expectations? An efficient project means that it is completed "just-in-time." If the project is completed early, that means that too many resources were dedicated to it, which would have caused a shortage of resources on other projects. If a project was completed late, that means that not enough resources were dedicated to it. The expression "efficient operations" means that all projects have just the right resources to be completed "just-in-time." The operations analysis should also identify how well staff members have been trained to operate efficiently. Are staff members able to prioritize tasks and avoid "fire-fighting"? A production efficiency analysis should work to identify areas of waste and locate operational bottlenecks.

Consider the following example. A staff engineer spends 20 hours over 3 days preparing calculations for a project. After completing the calculations, the staff engineer sends the calculations to a senior engineer for review. The senior engineer doesn't get a chance to review the calculations for 2 days. He then spends 2 hours reviewing the calculations and providing feedback. The staff engineer then spends 3 hours revising the calculations and sends them back to the senior engineer. After 2 more days, the senior engineer reviews the calculations for another hour and provides additional feedback. The staff engineer then spends 2 more hours making revisions and sends the calculations back to the senior engineer. The senior engineer then sends the calculations to the engineer responsible for stamping. After 4 days and 3 hours of review time, the engineer in charge provides feedback to the staff engineer, which includes several changes regarding the scope of the project. The staff engineer then spends 6 hours revising the calculations and sends them back to the engineer in charge and cc's the senior engineer. After 4 more days, the staff engineer follows up with the engineer in charge to determine if the calculations are approved and stamped. Two days later, the engineer in charge sends the stamped calculations to the staff engineer.

In this example, the inefficiencies of the firm's operations resulted in nearly 45% wasted time. This wasted time resulted in an extra cost of more than $1,500. This cost is covered by the firm, the client, or both. It took the firm 17 days to produce a final product, which could have been produced in 4 days if the waste and delays were eliminated. Unfortunately, this type of scenario is not uncommon.

Taken from a "Lean" perspective, the total amount of time spent on the project was 17 days times 8 hours per day or 136 hours. The amount of time spent actually working on the project was 37 hours. The total waste of time was 99 hours or 73%. The goal should be 37 hours, but in the lean world, even that would be too much since there are probably inefficiencies in the way the work itself was performed.

Let us give you a real example where this level of overly excessive control seriously damaged performance. This one occurred in the purchasing office of one of the world's largest oil and gas conglomerates. In this case, because of a history of inaccurate purchase orders, a series of controls were put in place to ensure that all purchase orders were properly vetted. A purchase order now required 16 approval signatures before it could be released.

The process of routing this document often took 6–8 months. Our role as consultants to this organization was to streamline the process, and we started by asking each of the 16 signees what they looked for on the document to determine whether to sign it. We were surprised when every one of the 16 told us that all they looked for was that another specific individual had signed the document. If so, they were sure the purchase order had to be correct.

In the end, they had 16 control points for every purchase order, all of which created waste, time delay, and none of which added value, because none of them actually checked the document. The failed system drove this behavior because it caused a false sense of security for all the signees. It would have been better to have one control point where the document was looked at carefully. Then, there would be more accuracy and significantly less waste.

Every organization has waste. That means that if a company is making a profit, the cost of the waste is then being passed on to the consumer. Every time you buy something, you are paying the cost of the item or service plus the cost of the waste. Every time a client hires your firm, part of what the client is paying for is waste. The level of waste of service providers is typically believed to range from 30% to 80%. I would argue that AEC firms are most likely at the higher end of that range.

To identify inefficiencies in operations, take the time to observe without saying a thing. Observe people working at different levels of the organization. Observe meetings, training, and orientations. Review projects and look for budget overruns and delays. In addition to observation, take the time to interview employees at various levels of the organization. Ask about the workflow and bottlenecks. Ask about sources of delays and sources of stress and frustration. Also, ask what efficient operations should look like to determine whether employees know how to eliminate waste and whether they have been provided the necessary direction and resources to do so.

4.4.2 Quality

An evaluation of quality is not just about looking at the final product or the delivery of the service to determine if it "looks good." More so, it's about evaluating how the organization achieves quality and how consistently quality is occurring. It's also about determining if members of the organization have a clear and common understanding of what quality looks like and how to achieve it. Each employee must clearly understand how his or her actions are contributing to the overall quality of the product being produced or the services being provided. Essentially, it must be determined if there is a consistent theme of quality throughout the process.

A great first step in this type of analysis is to ask many individuals at every level of the organization what quality is and how to achieve it. Undoubtedly, you will find many different ideas of quality and many different approaches to achieve quality. Ask yourself, if the members of the organization don't agree on what quality is, then how can the organization possibly determine if quality is being achieved? To take this analysis approach further, try asking some of your major clients what they consider to be a quality product or a quality service. Ask them what is most important to them when they hire an AEC firm. In most cases, the authors have found that not only does the organization not have a common understanding of quality, but also most organizations are completely out-of-touch with what the client considers to be a quality product or a quality service.

An analysis of the organization's quality should also include an evaluation of the approach to quality. Most AEC firms will ensure quality by looking at the final product. They will look at the finished drawings, calculations, or a completed task in the construction process to determine if it is good enough. This approach to quality results in a huge amount of time being wasted in reworking and revising. An effective approach to quality should apply "quality at the source" ideology. This means that quality is ensured as the work is being done, not just at the end of the process. It means that quality exists at every step. By the time the final product is ready, quality should be a guarantee because of the quality of the process, not because of a final review.

4.4.3 Cost

Cost is important, but far too often, too much emphasis is placed on this metric. Most costs, like inventory cost or cost of operations, are symptoms of a much larger problem. The ultimate goal of all operations should be the elimination of all non-value-added costs, which includes inventory costs and costs of operations. For example, in the United States, we tend to treat setup costs as something that we average out over a larger volume of products produced. One interesting example, which dates back several years, is a metal fender forming machine that was used by the United States, Sweden, and Japan. In the United States, the setup time for this machine was around 10 hours because it involved fork lifts, cranes, and lots of bolts.

Batch sizes were several hundred fenders for each setup, thereby averaging the setup time over all the items produced. Using this same machine, Sweden was able to drive the setup time down to 2 hours. In Japan, they were able to drive this setup time down to 12 minutes. Why the difference? Because Japan considered the inventory of hundreds of fenders to be more expensive. In Japan, they devised a swivel system that allowed the dies to be swung into place and then bolted down with just a few levers. Cost is an important measure, but rather than taking it as a given, we need to consider its elements of waste.

4.4.4 Value Stream

The value stream analysis is an evaluation of the workflow process that the organization follows to arrive at a final product. It follows the process step-by-step from start to finish and distinguishes the activities that create value for the client from those that do not create value. The analysis is useful for highlighting aspects of the workflow process that are waste and can be eliminated. By removing the waste from the process, the organization can complete projects with higher efficiency and ultimately increase the profit produced by each project.

There are some basic requirements that all processes should adhere to. These come from tools that are found in the Lean and Six Sigma worlds of the Toyota Production System (TPS) and there are entire books that describe these tools. The key tools are:

- 5S – This is a tool that says your workplace should be clean, organized, and safe. If you are not currently using the 5S tool, you are not ready to clean up your value stream.
- Standard Work – This tool says that there is a standard, documented way of doing the work. If everyone does it differently, then it can't be fixed. There needs to be a standard procedure before we can make improvements on the standard.
- Value Stream Mapping – This tool lays out the details of every step in the process. It documents value-added vs non-value-added time for each of the steps. It then looks for ways to reduce the non-value-added times. It is not focused on making employees work harder or faster; it is focused on improving the flow and preventing unnecessary steps, thereby working smarter.

A book that you may want to consider, which teaches these and many other Lean tools, is *Strategic Continuous Process Improvement: Which Quality Tools to Use, and When to Use Them.* McGraw-Hill, New York, 2012.

4.4.5 Financial Performance

An analysis of the financial performance of an organization is meant to evaluate the financial health of the organization as well as identify potential areas that can be improved. The financial health is typically not difficult to determine. However, identifying areas that can be improved may be more difficult. Improvement areas may include reducing unnecessary expenses and stabilizing cash flow. The financial performance analysis should also consider how well the organization is responding to financial stress. When profits begin to decrease, are there indicators set in place that will trigger actions to respond to financial conditions? Many organizations will keep a close eye on financial data but will not have action-oriented triggers set in place to maintain positive financial performance. The financial performance analysis should determine how quickly and effectively the organization is able to respond to changing financial conditions.

As mentioned earlier in our discussion of leading and lagging indicators, most financial performance focuses on lagging indicators, like KPIs (Key Performance Indicators) telling us, and the rest of the world, what we have done in the past, but giving us little guidance ahead of time to prevent problems. Leading indicators, when used properly, help us take corrective action and, therefore, help us improve the performance of our KPIs.

4.4.6 Commercial Performance

The commercial performance analysis evaluates how well the organization can conduct marketing and sales efforts. It considers the return on investment of marketing efforts and identifies the most profitable marketing activities. The analysis should also evaluate the consistency of marketing efforts. It is common for organizations to increase marketing efforts when work is slow and then reduce marketing efforts when work is busy. This approach results in the "feast or famine" routine that so many AEC organizations experience. Also, determine if your organization has an effective client relationship management plan. Is the plan being executed? Does it appear to be sufficient or does it need revising?

4.4.7 Continuous Improvement

An evaluation of continuous improvement refers to what the company has set in place to ensure that continuous improvement is happening. What steps has the company taken and what systems have been established to make sure that issues are addressed, not ignored? It is common for staff engineers to have a clear understanding of what the issues are because they are the ones in the trenches dealing with them. It is also common for staff to have great ideas of what improvements can be made. Unfortunately, most of the complaints and ideas the staff have are never communicated, resulting in lost opportunities for continuous improvement. Determine if there are systems in place for issues and ideas to be reported, evaluated, and addressed. If there are systems in place, determine if the staff concerns and ideas are taken seriously or if the system of reporting issues and ideas is more of a way to just make the staff feel they're being listened to. Evaluate if the existing systems are effective.

Continuous improvement also includes problem solving. Determine whether your organization has developed a problem-solving methodology and whether staff and managers have been trained to use problem-solving techniques and tools. If a problem-solving methodology has been developed, is it effective? Are problems addressed quickly or are problems allowed to persist? Are problems dealt with at the source or are they passed down the line? Also, determine if continuous improvement is engrained in the culture. Has every employee been empowered to contribute to continuous improvement?

4.5 DIFFERENTIATION ANALYSIS

Strategic differentiation is what makes your organization unique from your competitors. It goes beyond what your organization is good at and considers what your organization is the best at. A great way to think about differentiation is by asking what services your organization provides that your clients are willing to pay a premium for. What is your organization so good at that your clients will pay a higher fee to have you provide the service? If your clients will pay more for a specific service you provide, then you have differentiated yourself from your competitors in that service.

The analysis involves first determining if your organization has achieved strategic differentiation in any way. Then, identify opportunities for the organization to achieve strategic differentiation or enhance the differentiation it has already established. Achieving differentiation is only the first step. If it is not enhanced, it will be lost.

4.6 EMPLOYEE DEVELOPMENT ANALYSIS

The employees are the most valuable asset your organization has and their development is critical to every avenue for success. The best investment an organization can make to enhance their professional services offering is to dedicate time and resources to the training and education of their employees. Too many organizations avoid investing in their employees because they fear being taken advantage of. They fear that the employees will simply take the training and go to another organization. Henry Ford said, "The only thing worse than training your employees and having them leave is not training them and having them stay." Employees should be treated as long-term investments even though there is a risk they might leave. Investing in your employees not only makes them better at what they do, it also makes them more likely to stay with the organization longer because they recognize the value of the training and education they will receive. After all, if an employee's job with your organization is not enhancing his or her career, then why not do that same job for any other organization? What's the benefit of sticking around? Every aspect of the organization can be enhanced by investing in employees, including productivity, quality, customer service, marketing, etc. Additionally, when an organization values its employees and treats them as valuable assets, those employees will naturally treat clients in the same regard.

An effective employee development analysis should focus on employee development plans. Does every employee have an employee development plan and are the employees making progress towards accomplishing their goals? Is the organization supporting employees in their development? Identify areas of the employee development program that can be improved and what the organization can do to enhance the program. A corporate strategic plan is never complete until it embraces the value of employee development.

4.7 SUMMARY

The internal analysis is a critical self-evaluation of the organization's state of well-being. It focuses on identifying the internal root-causes of external symptoms to develop long-term solutions. It considers multiple perspectives, identifies the employees as valuable assets, and understands the powerful impact of corporate culture. Every external achievement begins with an internal improvement.

5

External Analysis

5.1 INTRODUCTION

An external analysis focuses on what is happening in the marketplace in which the firm is operating. It is an outward-looking analysis that evaluates environmental influences affecting the organization and compares the firm to the competition. Often, this type of analysis is best performed by an external organization, the main reason being that "you don't know what you don't know" – you don't know what to look for in the comparison analysis.

5.2 CLIENT RELATIONSHIP ANALYSIS

One of the most critical and perhaps most neglected type of analysis an Architectural, Engineering, and Construction (AEC) firm can perform is a client relationship analysis. Firms often focus primarily on financial and performance analyses and neglect to recognize the fact that without committed clients, the firm will fail. Clients often prefer to work with the firm they have the best relationship with, despite any shortcomings the firm may have. This has a lot to do with the culture of the organization, which will be discussed in more detail in the chapter on the Shingo Principles. Maintaining positive relationships with clients is a critical aspect of any effective strategy for service-providing organizations, such as engineering firms. The following are recommended steps to analyze the relationship a firm currently has with its clients:

- Identify the client
- Understand the client

5.2.1 Identify the Client

Before the client relationship can be analyzed, the client must first be identified. Who is the client? At first, the answer to this question may seem obvious. However, asking this question to a team of professionals all working on the same project will most likely result in multiple differing responses. As an example, consider a project to perform structural engineering services for a new hospital. Who is the client? Some will say the client is the architectural firm that hired the engineering firm as a sub-consultant. Others will say the client is the specific architect managing the project. Others may identify the owner of the new hospital or the owner's project manager in charge of construction of the new hospital. Some may identify the client to be those who will work in the hospital or perhaps the patients who will visit the hospital. Others may claim that the contractor using the structural drawings developed by the engineering firm is the client. This example illustrates the potential challenge of identifying who the client is.

In many cases, the client may not be the individual or organization that the invoice is sent to when the services are completed. Often, the individual receiving the invoice is another service provider but not the ultimate client. The challenge for an AEC firm is that the ultimate client may be an individual that the project team may never have any contact with. If the project team members do not have a common understanding of who the client is, they will have a difficult time developing a final product or providing a service that satisfies the needs and concerns of the client.

Because the client is often so far removed from the design team, the professionals working on the project must keep the client in mind. If the design team does not keep the client in mind, the project team may not produce a design that best creates value for the client. As an example, a bridge to nowhere does not provide value to its users no matter how elegant the engineering calculations may be. Calculations alone produce no value. Calculations applied to the needs of the client can produce significant value.

So, what about the other organizations and individuals providing services in the example of the structural engineering firm working on the hospital? What about the architect managing the project or the contractor using the engineered drawings? Although not the client, these individuals and organizations deserve special consideration as well. These are all in the Supply Chain of the overall project and are stakeholders in the success of the project. Engineered designs must comply with the architectural intent and must satisfy the constructability requirements of the contractor. However, keeping the client in mind while working with other service providers helps prevent the compounding effects of mistakes. If one service provider creates a design that does not provide value to the client, the other service providers are at a risk of adding to the design flaw. By considering the needs of the ultimate client, design flaws can be corrected, instead of being amplified.

5.2.2 Understand the Client

Once the client has been identified, the client must be understood. In many cases, understanding the client may not be difficult because the professionals working on the project team have experience acting as the client. If, for example, a design team is performing engineering services for a new shopping center, the engineers on the design team have undoubtedly been patrons of shopping centers themselves. However, in some cases, it may be difficult for the design team to truly understand the needs of the client. The needs of cardiac patients in a hospital, for example, may be completely unknown to the engineers on the design team.

Gaining an understanding of the needs of the client can be achieved in many ways and, often, a thorough understanding requires the use of more than one approach. The design team should conduct interviews or surveys to better understand the needs of the client. The design team should discuss client needs with other service providers and professionals to better understand past mistakes and anticipate future needs. In some cases, historical data may provide the design team with a better understanding of the needs of the client. The critical point here is that the design team must take the time to understand the needs of the client. It is important to understand the project from the point of view of the client and not just the points of view of the other service providers. Avoid the temptation to jump into the project before understanding the problem that is supposed to be solved.

5.3 SUPPLY CHAIN ANALYSIS

A Supply Chain can best be exemplified by an old Chinese proverb, which says that it takes 10,000 people to make bread. In this example, you have the person who sells the bread, but behind that person is:

- the one who delivers the bread
- the one who bakes the bread

- the store that sells the grain
- the one who collects the ingredients
- the miller who mills the grain
- the farmer who grows the grain
- the farmer who milks the cow
- the toolmaker who makes the shovel
- the steel smith who makes the steel
- the carpenter who makes the handle
- the logger who cuts the tree
- the toolmaker who makes the saw
- the stonemason who cuts the grindstone
- the builder who builds the mill
- the seamstress who makes the uniforms
- the carver who makes the buttons
- the weaver who makes the cloth
- the weaver who makes the thread
- and so on!

From this example, we see why it takes 10,000 people to make a loaf of bread. And every one of these individuals is important in the overall process. No one is unimportant or insignificant in this supply chain. Everyone deserves the respect that their performance and participation deserve. For us, the lesson is that we need to pay attention to the entire Supply Chain as we approach operational efficiency. Missing just one piece can bring the entire project to a sudden and complete halt.

The supply chain for an AEC firm is the system of linkages between all of the different service providers involved in a project. This may include an architectural firm, a surveying company, multiple engineering firms, a general contractor with subcontractors, and possibly a project management firm. All these service providers may be thought of and referred to as internal customers, process partners, or simply members of the supply chain. An analysis of the supply chain focuses on the following main areas:

- Relationship Analysis
- Supply Chain Analysis

5.3.1 Relationship Analysis

Relationship analysis involves gaining an understanding of the expectations and frustrations of the other service providers included in the supply chain. Maintaining positive relationships can be fundamental to the success of projects as well as vital to obtaining future work. Poor relationships between members of the supply chain can often result in schedule delays, budget overruns, and lawsuits. Synergistic relationships between members of the supply chain can result in increases in effectiveness, efficiency, profitability, and client satisfaction.

It is common for AEC firms to value their relationship with those in the supply chain that typically select the firm for projects. However, they often undervalue their relationship with service providers that do not select the firm. For example, an engineering firm may value their relationship with the architect or the project manager who hired them but may not give much attention to their relationship with the contractor. An analysis of relationships with other members of the supply chain must include all members of the supply chain, not just the ones who are able to provide future work.

One of the best ways to analyze a firm's relationship with other members of the supply chain is through surveys and interviews. A survey or interview can provide the firm with feedback about an array of relationship issues. It can give the firm a better understanding of what the most important aspects of the relationships being analyzed are and how relationships can be improved. It can also create an opportunity for other service providers to get frustrations off their chest.

When preparing for a survey, the format in which the survey is administered should be carefully considered. Surveys can be conducted in person, over the phone, online, or by sending out a form and requesting responses. Different formats may be more attractive to different members of the supply chain and may be more likely to result in honest survey responses. In many cases, the best way to conduct a survey may be an informal lunch meeting during which the survey questions are asked and responses are discussed in order to gain a full understating of the point of view of the one being surveyed. Whether administered in person or by other means, the designer of the survey should carefully consider which format will result in honest and constructive feedback.

The questions asked during a survey should be thoughtfully constructed. The questions should be as concise and as few as possible. Avoid asking multiple questions that essentially provide similar feedback. The survey should include open-ended questions that promote an explanation of the answer, rather than a simple yes or no. Questions should seek insight into weaknesses as well as strengths. Knowing what a firm's strengths are is just as valuable as identifying any weaknesses. The survey should also be designed in a way that will result in measurable data. The same questions should be asked of everyone surveyed to create comparable results. One way to construct survey questions so that the responses provide measurable data, as well as an explanation of the response, is as follows:

> On a scale of 0 to 10, how would you rate our firm's responsiveness and why would you give our firm that rating?

A common tool to use during a survey is the Net Promoter Score (NPS). NPS provides measurable data indicating how likely those being surveyed are to recommend your firm's services. NPS is a simple tool that involves asking the following question:

> On a scale of 0 to 10, how likely are you to recommend our firm's services to a valued colleague?

The responses from 0 to 10 are then ranked into three categories. Responses ranging from 0 to 6 are considered "Detractors," which are the individuals who would be most likely tell a valued colleague not to use your firm. Responses ranging from 7 to 8 are considered "Passives," which are the individuals who would not recommend your firm to a valued colleague but would also not tell them not to use your firm. Responses ranging from 9 to 10 are considered "Promoters," which are the individuals who would recommend your firm to a valued colleague. The NPS is then calculated as follows:

$$NPS = \frac{\left(\#\,of\,Promoters\right) - \left(\#\,of\,Detractors\right)}{Total\,\#\,of\,Respondents} \times 100$$

NPS is a percentage indicating how likely those surveyed are to promote your firm's services. A high NPS suggests that those surveyed are "evangelists" for your firm or that they are likely to actively promote your services to others. A firm with a high NPS will be more likely to obtain a significant number of new clients by referral rather than by marketing campaigns. The NPS can provide valuable insight into the overall health of current relationships. However, NPS should not be used alone. The NPS does not highlight strengths and weaknesses. It provides a snapshot of how a firm is doing but does not provide data about specific problem areas that can be used to make strategic improvements. For this reason, the NPS should be used in conjunction with additional survey questions.

5.3.2 Supply Chain Analysis

The supply chain for an AEC firm consists of all the suppliers of services, materials, technologies, and information that contribute to the completion of a project. The analysis of the supply chain evaluates every aspect of the process to identify potential areas of improvement, such as bottlenecks, budget overruns, product deficiencies, and more. The analysis of the supply chain can lead to improvements that can often result in significant competitive advantages. Improving the supply chain can result in faster delivery times, increased profits, and increased client satisfaction. Conducting a supply chain analysis is common for manufacturing companies but is not commonly used in service industries like the AEC industry. As a result, AEC firms that take advantage of opportunities to improve their supply chains can make advances that other firms will continue to miss out on. The most common first step in conducting a supply chain analysis is by developing a supply chain map to identify potential opportunities for improvement. Chart 5.1 shows an example of the supply chain for a bedsheet. Even something as simple as a sheet can have enormous complexities.

5.4 SWOT ANALYSIS

A SWOT analysis is a common tool used to organize a firm's strengths, weaknesses, opportunities, and threats into an easy-to-understand visual matrix. One of the primary values of performing a SWOT analysis is that it creates a focused dialogue between members of the analysis team. It forces firms to ask hard questions and discuss different points of view.

Although the SWOT analysis evaluates both internal and external aspects of the organization, it is included in the external analysis simply because it is critical that the analysis team remembers that the SWOT analysis is a comparative analysis. The results of the analysis must be considered relative to the firm's competition and the needs of the client. As an example, to explain this concept, imagine the owner of a design firm has marketing materials produced that state that one of the firm's strengths

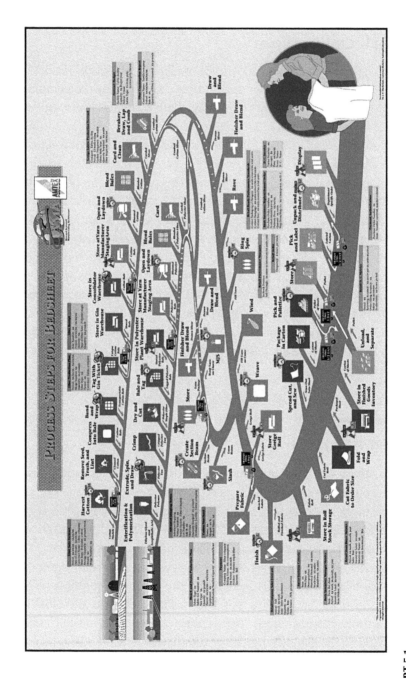

CHART 5.1
Bedsheet supply chain.

is fast turnaround time. The owner of the design firm truly believes that this is one of the firm's most impressive strengths. However, the firm's project managers know that the clients often complain that projects seem to always fall behind schedule and that other firms seem to produce drawings faster. In this case, the owner performed an internal analysis of the firm's strengths and considered turnaround time to be a strength. However, when the firm's turnaround time is compared to the competition and the opinion of the client is taken into consideration, turnaround time is no longer a strength but, in fact, should be considered a weakness. For this reason, the SWOT analysis must be treated as a comparative analysis where the results are relative to competing firms and the needs of the client. A SWOT analysis that is not a relative comparison may not be accurate.

The strengths and weaknesses are discussed by the analysis team and are listed in the appropriate cells of the SWOT matrix. The discussion of strengths and weaknesses must be an open and honest discussion that compares the firm to competitors. A strength is not a true strength unless the firm is better at it than its competitors. The analysis team should consider the firm's strengths and weaknesses relating to the quality of submittals, the quality of customer service, and the efficiency of processes. What does the firm do exceptionally well and why do clients choose your firm over others? What are the things that clients complain about and what are the things that you respect about other firms?

Opportunities refer to the things that the company is currently not doing but perhaps should be doing. A great way to identify opportunities is to discuss challenges and issues that continue to arise. An example would be a civil engineering firm that continues to experience project delays because the surveying companies take too long to provide the necessary survey data. The civil engineering firm may look at this issue and consider hiring its own in-house surveyors to prevent the delays caused by hiring survey companies to do the surveying.

Threats refer to harmful trends or changes in the market that cannot be avoided. These are the issues that a firm must plan and prepare for. Threats may include changes in the economy, the introduction of new competition, or the loss of a regular client. The difference between a threat and an opportunity is that a threat is an issue that cannot reasonably be turned into an opportunity. The following figure illustrates the typical layout of the SWOT analysis matrix (Chart 5.2).

Strengths	Weaknesses
• _____	• _____
• _____	• _____
• _____	• _____
• _____	• _____
• _____	• _____
Opportunities	Threats
• _____	• _____
• _____	• _____
• _____	• _____
• _____	• _____
• _____	• _____

CHART 5.2
SWOT analysis.

5.5 PESTLE ANALYSIS

A pestle analysis is a type of market analysis. It focuses on key market factors which are political, economic, social, technological, legislative, and environmental (PESTLE). The PESTLE analysis may require some research and consultation with other professionals in the market. When conducting a PESTLE analysis, consider both confirmed trends and potential trends and list questions that cannot currently be answered.

Political market factors and trends may include changes in funding for government projects or changes in political views that could affect how AEC firms do business. Economic market factors may include economic growth or decline, taxation changes, or changes in interest rates that may affect the demand for AEC services. Social market factors may include consumer views, media views, or major social events that may affect the society's perception of the firm's operations, marketing campaigns, and what is considered best practice. Technological market factors may include software and hardware advances as well as research into AEC advances that may affect the firm's operations. Legislative market factors may include changes in laws, regulations, codes, and licensing requirements. Environmental market factors may include seasonal climate impacts on operations as well as ecological concerns that may create challenges or

Political	• _____ • _____ • _____
Economic	• _____ • _____ • _____
Social	• _____ • _____ • _____
Technological	• _____ • _____ • _____
Legislative	• _____ • _____ • _____
Environmental	• _____ • _____ • _____

CHART 5.3
PESTLE analysis.

opportunities for engineering firms. The above figure illustrates a typical layout of a PESTLE analysis matrix (Chart 5.3).

5.6 GAP ANALYSIS

A gap analysis evaluates the firm's current performance level, compares it to the desired performance level, and develops potential actions that could bridge the gap between actual performance and desired performance. The gap analysis utilizes aspects of both the SWOT analysis and the PESTLE analysis but develops them even further and promotes a discussion about what success looks like.

A gap analysis evaluates all aspects of the firm including the quality of submittals, the efficiency of operations, the effectiveness of marketing campaigns, relationships with clients, etc. The desired performance levels must be realistic but optimistic and may require some research into the performance levels of competitors. At this point, the action items do not need to be fully developed into objectives or goals but should be considered "potential" actions. The following figure illustrates a typical gap analysis matrix template (Chart 5.4).

Current status	Potential actions	Desired status
1-	•_____ •_____ •_____	
2-	•_____ •_____ •_____	
3-	•_____ •_____ •_____	

CHART 5.4
Gap analysis.

5.7 INDEPENDENT EXTERNAL ASSESSMENTS

As mentioned earlier, independent external assessments are more expensive, but also more valuable than assessments performed by internal staff members. There are numerous reasons why, but one reason has already been highlighted:

- You don't know what you don't know. External assessments should introduce "experts" who have a broader background and hopefully have experience in numerous industry sectors, thereby allowing them to make suggestions which would normally not even be on the radar of an internal assessment.
- An independent perspective, as opposed to an ingrained corporate perspective, offers the freedom to say things that may not be considered politically correct when viewed from inside the organization.
- A good, independent assessment will raise a different set of questions. It will identify opportunities that insiders didn't even consider.
- A good, independent assessment should be able to identify the "Big Gaps" which an insider might miss. It's the "can't see the forest for the trees" syndrome. The external assessor should also be able to link the gaps to the enterprise priorities.
- An independent assessor should be able to prioritize the gaps using tools like the Impact/Effort Matrix and thereby help the enterprise focus their efforts accordingly.

An excellent external assessment that focuses on comparing the culture of your organization with others is available at www.shingoprize.org/insight.

5.8 SUMMARY

An external analysis evaluates environmental challenges and opportunities and assesses how the strengths and weaknesses of the organization will affect its ability to face external challenges. The Japanese organizational theorist Kenichi Ohmae said: "Rowing harder doesn't help if the boat is headed in the wrong direction." An external analysis will contribute to the organization's ability to determine if they are heading in the right direction.

Phase II

Define: Establishing the Best Path to the Ideal Future State

6

Introduction to Define

6.1 INTRODUCTION

An example of shifting cultures and shifting behaviors was found in a hospital project in which the author was involved. In this case, the hospital president and his senior staff were directed by their board to come up with a strategic plan. The board was frustrated by the long wait times and high costs of hospital operation and they wanted to get it under control. Potential patients preferred to go to nearby hospitals which were more responsive to the patients' needs. The hospital leadership was directed to put a focus on improving customer quality and cost reduction.

The author led the strategy workshops, which were a series of half-day workshops each week over a month. A preferred off-site 2-day option was deemed unacceptable. However, the space between the sessions worked to the advantage of the author in that it allowed intermediate time for data collection. In the end, the weekly meetings continued well past the 2 months.

The leadership was convinced that what they needed to do was focus on cost and run some RIEs (Lean Rapid Improvement Events) on the stockrooms, and that this would identify where cost waste was occurring. The author disagreed. He challenged them to focus first on customer satisfaction by identifying where customer failures were occurring, and he affirmed that costs would be reduced by first focusing on the hospital's culture and their attitude about customer satisfaction. He stressed that by looking at cost as a higher priority than customer satisfaction exemplified that the culture of the hospital was pointed in the wrong direction. A strategic plan was developed with a primary focus on the customer.

The author challenged the leadership to start by focusing on customer satisfaction, commencing with their highest priced real estate, which would also be their highest failure point. This, of course, was the OR (operating room). They were currently using a scheduling methodology for the OR where doctors blocked off a segment of time and this time period was locked up for that doctor, no matter how little of that time he or she actually utilized. In conjunction with the leadership of the hospital, a scheduling system was redesigned that would allow smaller time segments which were specific to the procedure that would be performed. Using a gemba (Go and Observe) approach, they also realized that a lot of what was done in the OR could be done outside of the OR either before or after the procedure. By making these changes, and after about 3 months of using the new scheduling methodology, the hospital tripled the amount of procedures that were being run through the OR, significantly reducing the cost of each procedure and significantly increasing utilization and capacity.

The strategy team moved on to the next most expensive real estate in the hospital, which was the ER (emergency room). Similar gemba observations of the ER quickly identified that the delays in the ER were primarily caused by a lack of responsiveness by the labs and also a lack of efficiency in scheduling beds in the main hospital. The patients would be on hold in the ER for hours waiting for lab work or waiting for a bed. And this made turnaround in the ER very slow. The gemba focused on studying the lab systems and the bed scheduling systems. In the end, the poor performance of these systems was the result of the labs and bed schedulers not knowing the impact that they were having on the ER. They didn't see the big picture. No one was watching the performance of the overall ER flow and the systems connected with that flow. Once again, now that the big system perspective had been identified and appropriate changes were made to the systems, performance was dramatically affected. Wait time in the ER was reduced, in the worst-case scenario, from hours to minutes. The ER soon prided itself on trying to keep the wait times down to single-digit minutes.

The big change that occurred was in the culture. Hospital leadership no longer focused on cost reduction, previously thinking of themselves as a factory. They realized that customer satisfaction needed to be the focus. Along with this, the cultural transformation of the leadership trickled down to management and the associates. They felt more pride in their work when their customers were satisfied with the reduced response times and the improved results.

The author stepped out of this project at this point, which was about 6 months into the transformation effort, but the leadership continued their weekly strategy meetings and made that a permanent part of their new culture, and then continued working on different systems within the hospital.

Another interesting case in strategically "missing the mark" is the NASA Space Shuttle. Was it a failure, or wasn't it? Originally, the shuttle was to go into space six or more times a year. In the end, it was less than one time a year. The difference that was missed in the strategy was in the requirement for safety checks that had to be performed between flights. Each manufacturer of a component was required to create a list of areas requiring inspection between flights. And each of the inspection sheets must be completed. The inspections, in and of themselves, were a good thing. However, the redundancies were enormous, and each redundant test had to be performed separately for each inspection sheet. Doing an inspection one time in order to satisfy all the times the inspection was required wasn't acceptable because the inspections were performed by different teams. The various inspections could require minutes to days to complete. The accumulative time required by all the redundant inspections increased the lead time between flights to the point where the space shuttle program was considered to be a financial failure in that it didn't accomplish the desired number of trips each year. It couldn't be cost justified. You could say that quality killed the space shuttle program. In reality, the reason for the space shuttle's financial failure was a lack of strategic planning and achieving visibility regarding the big picture.

Following the process that we observed in the previous chapters, and having thoroughly analyzed the current situation, many of the needed outcomes of the strategy are most likely becoming obvious. The Define Phase will use the results of the internal and external analyses to develop a strategy that, when executed properly, will effectively drive the organization in the desired direction.

As the strategic planning team approaches this phase, keep in mind that the process of defining the strategy is just as important as the resulting defined strategy. Avoid the temptation to simply fill out an online strategy template or reuse an old ineffective strategy. Taking the time to go through the process of defining the strategy will not only result in a more effective strategy but will also begin the process of engaging the entire organization in the successful execution of the strategy.

6.2 WHY DEFINE?

As you've worked to conduct an analysis of the organization, many issues have hopefully been discussed in detail. Think about some of the issues that have been discussed and consider what the origins of these issues might have been. For example, maybe one of the issues that has been discussed is an unsatisfactory level of quality of submittals. This issue might have developed over time due to a lack of attention to quality. Now, consider how this issue might have been prevented if an effective strategy had been defined in the past. As you think through the existing issues, it should be easy to see how a well-defined strategy might have prevented them. Defining your strategy works to develop solutions to existing issues and helps us prepare for potential upcoming challenges. Although there are many reasons for defining the strategy, the primary reasons are to establish clear direction, develop strategic thinking, and enhance buy-in.

6.2.1 Establish Clear Direction

The first purpose for defining a strategy is to establish clear direction for the organization. Too often, employees and organizational units unknowingly work hard to move the organization in opposing directions, turning their efforts into a tug-of-war instead of forward momentum. Without organization-wide direction, the decision-making processes of managers is focused purely on what is best for their own unit but may not necessarily be what is best for the organization as a whole. Hard work, lacking a clear and united vision, may result in an organization running in circles. The establishment of a clear direction allows the strategy to be more dynamic and agile. The strategy will have the ability to be applied to all organizational units and will have the agility to adapt to changing conditions. When decision makers throughout the organization have a clear understanding of where the organization is heading, they will be more likely to make decisions that work to accomplish a common mission, rather than work against each other. Additionally, managers will be able to make decisions quickly and will have enthusiastic confidence in their decision, knowing that their decisions are aligned with a united direction.

6.2.2 Develop Strategic Thinking

An agile organization is one that has established a culture of problem solving and cohesive decision making. Defining the strategy is not just about the resulting strategic plan. The process of defining the plan develops strategic thinking within the organization that helps decision makers apply the strategy to their unit's specific operational challenges and limitations. A strategic plan that is not accompanied by a culture of strategic thinking is akin to a construction company that owns powerful machinery that none of the employees know how to use. Taking the time to clearly define the strategy is like writing a user manual for the machinery. It's the first step to making the strategy usable.

6.2.3 Enhance Buy-In

During the Analyze Phase, buy-in was initiated by applying the perspectives of individuals from various aspects of the organization. As we move into the Define Phase, it is critical that the buy-in that has been initiated is further enhanced. The Define Phase discussed in this book will work to strengthen buy-in and spread it to more individuals throughout the organization. Establishing and enhancing buy-in are an ongoing process and should be embedded into every aspect of the strategic planning process.

6.3 APPROACH TO DEFINE

The approach to defining the strategy presented in this phase revolves around making the strategy more executable. When the Define Phase is conducted effectively, the Execute Phase will be more likely to be implemented successfully as a natural result, rather than a forced next step. There are several aspects that should be included in the Define Phase which are outlined in the following image (see Chart 6.1).

CHART 6.1
Strategic Excellence Model – Define Phase.

6.4 SUMMARY

The AEC industry is full of individuals who are fantastic at identifying project challenges, design flaws, schedule delays, and the need for change orders and fee adjustments. However, the AEC professional who becomes highly valuable to the organizations and clients they work for are those who not only can identify problems but are able to maintain a focus on solutions. No client likes to be presented with a long list of issues and no solutions.

During the Analyze Phase, we focused on identifying the issues. During the Define Phase, we shift gears to developing solutions. An analysis of issues that does not result in effective solutions holds no value. Strategic thinking is all about solutions. Hard work with no vision is just work. Hard work applied to an inspired vision is innovation.

> Vision without action is merely a dream. Action without vision just passes the time. Vision with action can change the world.

> **Joel A. Barker**

7

Shingo Guiding Principles

7.1 INTRODUCTION

A principle is a result-oriented universal truth. "Result oriented" means that the result or the consequence of complying with or defying the principle will follow naturally and is unavoidable. For example, if you throw a rock up, it will come back down. The consequence is natural and unavoidable. "Universal truth" means that the principle will always hold true, even if we try to ignore it. For example, ignoring the falling rock simply means you may get hit on the head. Ignoring it doesn't change the universal truth associated with the principle.

7.2 GUIDING PRINCIPLES

In business, as in physics, we can find guiding principles. Discovering these principles and developing an understanding of them means that an organization can gain better control of the results associated with them. Knowing that the rock will come back down means you know better than to ignore it. In business, knowing the inevitable consequences of our actions can guide our behaviors and decision-making processes.

The guiding principles that will be discussed in this chapter have been carefully researched and developed over many years by the Shingo Institute at Utah State University in Logan, Utah. These principles can develop within an organization a powerful culture that will effectively promote ideal behaviors and ultimately, through the application of powerful strategic purpose and efficient organizational systems, produce ideal results. Each of the 10 guiding principles from the Shingo Institute will be discussed individually. The following image presents a summary of

CHART 7.1
Shingo Institute Guiding Principles.

the guiding principles and their organizational themes. This graphic was produced by the Shingo Institute and is available at www.shingoprize.org (Chart 7.1).

7.2.1 Respect Every Individual

Having respect for every individual doesn't just mean being polite. It's more than what you do, it's a state of being and an honest feeling towards others. Having respect for all individuals means that you truly respect who they are, how they feel, and what they think. You honestly value their opinions, their frustrations, and their expectations. It means that you show respect towards others because you sincerely feel respect for others, even those who can't do anything for you. How you treat others will often be the most pronounced aspect of your own personal brand.

Respecting other individuals will create in them positive feelings towards you and will make them more likely to work well with you. As you demonstrate that your respect towards them is true, they, in turn, will begin to respect you as well. As all the members of the organization adopt this guiding principle of respecting every individual, a culture of trust will prevail, resulting in a significant increase in synergy and problem solving. Additionally, employees who feel respected by the organization that they work for are more likely to demonstrate that same level of respect to the customers of the organization. The respectful culture of the organization will naturally spill outside of the organization and all stakeholders will recognize the culture and be appreciative of it.

A powerful way for an organization to respect every employee is to recognize everyone's value. Too many organizations still maintain the old industrial age thinking that employees are just another expense. Because of this thinking, most organizations are operating far below their potential simply because they don't allow their employees to truly apply all their intelligence, skills, and ambitions to perform their jobs. Employees are not an expense, they are the organization's most valuable asset, and they should be treated as such. Every employee should have a personal development plan, and the organization should be supporting its employees in the realization of those plans. Employees should be mentored, trained, and supported in their roles and they should be given opportunities to expand their knowledge and skill sets. Improvements made to operations should be heavily influenced by the employees who carry out the operations daily, and changes to operations should not just be enforced upon them by the management team. Truly great leaders can see the valuable potential in others and can empower them to make that potential a reality. Any organization that works to develop the full potential of its employees will enjoy higher performance than what was even believed to be possible.

Respecting every individual is a universally true principle. Employees that are respected by the organization they work for will perform beyond the expectations of the organization and will become loyal and highly prized assets that the organization will work hard to never lose. Stakeholders who are respected will become evangelists for the organization and will recommend the services of the organization to even their closest associates. An organization that truly respects every individual will, in turn, become respected by every individual.

7.2.2 Lead with Humility

True improvement begins with humility. Without humility, a leader will not be able to recognize his or her mistakes and weaknesses and, thus, will never be able to make the necessary improvements. Humility is the prerequisite to progress. When a leader lacks humility, he or she will miss opportunities to correct the course of the organization because pride will continue to drive the organization in the wrong direction, despite all the evidence indicating that the wrong course has been selected.

Leading with humility means you have an honest understanding that you can and will make mistakes. When a mistake is made, it means you own the mistake and you seek out and listen to the opinions of others as you work to correct the mistake. Leading with humility will drive you to recognize all mistakes – those that you make and those that others make – as opportunities to learn and improve. You will see the mistakes as not belonging to any individual but rather as belonging to the organization. More than 95% of the time, mistakes are the result of poor systems design, rather than poor people performance. There is an old lean principle that is often forgotten which states, "Design your systems so that the right thing is easier to do than the wrong thing." With that principle in mind, employees won't be caught short-cutting the system and there will be less finger pointing and more cooperation in solving problems.

Leading with humility will create a culture of problem solving. Employees will not hide their mistakes but will be comfortable to quickly make them known because they know their leader will work with them to find a solution. Leading with humility will help to eliminate the blame game and develop a team attitude of continuous improvement. C. S. Lewis said, "Humility is not thinking less of yourself, it's thinking of yourself less."

7.2.3 Seek Perfection

Seeking perfection may seem like an audacious goal. But it is the audacity of the goal that will drive the organization to accomplish what it did not think possible. It's not unlike an archer who aims his arrow up towards the sky. The archer doesn't actually expect to hit the sky. But it is by aiming high that the arrow can travel a greater distance. The same is true for an organization.

Seeking perfection will drive an organization to develop long-term solutions to problems, rather than just focusing on putting out fires or creating work-arounds, thereby making it work for now. Leaders of the organization will be more focused on ensuring that the organization continues to improve even after they are gone. Staff members will see the organization as a long-term career, rather than a short-term means to an end. Continuous improvement and the simplification of processes will become second nature. The true power in seeking perfection is not in the perfection; it is in the seeking because what is perfection today will not be perfection tomorrow. The seeking is eternal.

7.2.4 Focus on Process

Focusing on process means that when a problem occurs, leaders of the organization seek to solve the problem by improving the system that has harbored it. Too often, organizations work to solve problems by targeting an individual or a few individuals in order to place blame for the problem. If the problem is only solved with the individual, then the problem is only temporarily solved and will eventually recur. Problems must be resolved by improving the processes to prevent them from happening again.

To illustrate this principle, consider an engineering firm that is experiencing regular complaints from contractors about the poor quality of the drawings being produced. The engineering firm realizes that many of the complaints are resulting from drawings produced by one of the staff engineers. To solve the problem, the staff engineer is dismissed. However, the complaints continue. When the organization analyzes the current processes, it is discovered that the staff engineers are given generous bonuses based on how quickly they complete projects. As a result, the staff engineers are completing drawings as fast as possible with little concern for quality. It can be noted that the cause of the problem is in the processes, not the individual. The current processes do nothing to encourage quality drawings because staff engineers will get larger bonuses if they ignore quality and focus entirely on production speed. Even if all the staff engineers are replaced with new hires, the problem will persist because the processes have not been corrected.

Focusing on processes will result in true solutions to problems. It will reduce finger pointing and promote a collaborative approach to problem solving. It will create an organization that relies less on a few high-performing "rock stars" and, instead, is successful because of a high-performing system.

7.2.5 Embrace Scientific Thinking

Scientific thinking in a business setting is the application of the scientific method to decision making and problem solving. It's the analytical use of data to systematically determine the methods that are most likely to optimize outcomes. The scientific method is also used to test innovative ideas throughout the organization.

The application of scientific thinking in an organization means that problems are perceived as opportunities to improve. Many organizations throughout the AEC industry experience the same types of problems. The organizations that approach a problem using scientific thinking and treat the problem as an opportunity will overcome the problem and make advances whereas other organizations will continue to struggle with the problem. Likewise, organizations that embrace scientific thinking will develop innovative advances to their expertise and services.

A great approach to embracing scientific thinking in an AEC organization is to develop a structured approach to decision making, problem solving, and embracing new ideas. The members of the organization should be trained and regularly mentored in problem-solving methods, so that they feel comfortable using them. Problems should be approached with a positive attitude, and suggestions for innovative changes should be seriously explored using a structured process and should be appropriately applied.

7.2.6 Flow and Pull Value

Creating flow and pull value means that service capacity has the agility to respond to the customer's changing needs. It involves developing uninterrupted workflow by reducing waste and eliminating bottlenecks as well as having the right capacity to provide the services demanded by the customer without having excess capacity and unnecessary overhead.

Too often, the customer unknowingly pays for a significant amount of overhead because of inefficient flow. Projects often run over budget due to delays and complications created by operational inefficiencies within the organization. These budget overruns cause fees to go up and can even result in fee adjustments. When an organization takes the time to develop an operational flow that is designed to create value for the customer, projects are less likely to run over budget, thus allowing the AEC firm to pass those savings on to the client.

Additionally, having more control over flow allows the organization to have more control over project schedules and budgets, allowing the managers to have operational agility and to decrease the occurrence of "firefighting" exercises. This agility creates the ability to respond quickly to changes in customer demand by allowing customer needs to pull projects through the system on an as-needed basis. Pull value means that service capacity is responsive to the needs of the client. Operational agility will also help to smooth out the "feast or famine" experienced by so many organizations.

7.2.7 Assure Quality at the Source

Quality at the source means that any defects are identified and resolved as soon as they are created. It means that defects are not passed down the line and caught at the end. It means that quality is part of the process, instead of simply being a control or inspection step at the end of the process. When defects are caught at the end of a process, they require corrections and rework, thus costing extra time and resources to correct the error and revise any work that followed the error.

A great way to assure quality at the source is by organizing workflow in such a way that defects are identified throughout the process. The organization should also have a clear and common understanding of what quality means and how to achieve it. This approach creates a culture of quality that produces high-quality deliverables that did not require extensive reviewing and reworking at the end of the process. By the time a deliverable reaches the end of the process, the quality is already at a very high level.

7.2.8 Think Systematically

Thinking systematically involves gaining a thorough understanding of how all the different functions and phases of an organization's operations affect each other. It involves clear insight into how making a change to one aspect of the organization will influence operations throughout the rest of the organization.

Thinking systematically requires members of the organization to think about how their actions and decisions will affect others. It involves creating a clear flow of information and recommendations. Communication and transparency throughout the organization reduce unintended impacts on operations and prevent surprises. Thinking systematically also involves clear daily goals and visual management tools that allow teams to know if they are meeting operational expectations throughout the day.

7.2.9 Create Constancy of Purpose

Constancy of purpose means that all members of the organization have a clear and common understanding of the vision and mission of the organization. It means that the goals and efforts of the entire organization are aligned with the strategy. This type of constancy of purpose guides the decisions of managers and motivates the efforts of staff members.

A constancy of purpose not only guides the organization but also creates a higher level of confidence throughout the organization. It provides the organization with a foundational constitution that allows members of the organization to know who they are, what they stand for, and what they are working to achieve. This clarity of purpose and boost in confidence will act as a powerful driving force for marketers and business developers. It will also make decision making and problem solving less of a struggle because many of the solutions will become clear as the members of the organization work to align their decisions with the purpose of the organization. Ultimately, constancy of purpose will create a purpose-driven synergistic culture where all are working together to support a common vision.

7.2.10 Create Value for the Customer

Creating value for the customer means approaching every aspect of the business from the perspective of what's important to the client. It means rethinking each process with the client in mind. Too often, over years of operating, organizations develop large overhead costs due to overly complicated processes. The organization typically thinks of these costs as necessary; however, if the client knew what he was paying for, he may disagree.

A great way to create value for the customer is to evaluate each process with the client in mind. Think of what the client would be happy to pay for and which expenses would make the client consider moving his/her business to other organizations. It should be clear how each process is adding value for the client. There should also be a clear understanding of what is truly important to the client. This requires taking the time to understand the client and not just making assumptions. Organizations spend a significant amount of time doing things that the client doesn't actually care about. Refocusing efforts based on the priorities of the client can eliminate waste and provide a significant increase in value to the client, often at a reduced cost.

7.3 SUMMARY

The engineer and management consultant Joseph M. Juran said, "Without a standard there is no logical basis for making a decision or taking action."

Discover excellence (prerequisite)
Behaviors that lead to enterprise excellence

 Cultural enablers
Behaviors that enable a culture of respect and humility

 Continuous improvement
Behaviors that improve a continuous flow of value

 Enterprise alignment/results
Behaviors that align people, systems and strategy

 Build excellence
Driving strategy to execution

Five workshops . . . How principles inform

CHART 7.2
Shingo Institute Workshops.

The Shingo guiding principles act as that standard and when adopted by an organization, they will direct decision making at all levels of the organization. The Shingo Institute offers a series of highly recommended workshops that can help organizations develop a deep understanding of the guiding principles and provide instruction on how to apply them. The above figure is an outline of the available workshops that can be explored further at www.shingoprize.org/ (Chart 7.2). They also offer a book which introduces the basic insights and principles of the Shingo model and which can be purchased at all major outlets. The book focuses on the first course in this series and is titled *Discover Excellence: An Overview of the Shingo Model and Its Principles (The Shingo Model Series).*

8

Establishing a Direction

8.1 INTRODUCTION

In Chart 8.1a, we see an example of a table that was designed by the engineering department and then "thrown over the wall" for manufacturing to produce. This organization was siloed, and the engineers would never soil themselves by walking out into the production area or communicating with production employees.

A meeting was held to remove some of the silos and get departments to work more closely together. The company leadership discovered that there was a lot of waste generated in departments, like production, trying to work around the designs created by engineering who seemed to have no idea of the pain that they were causing. One of the topics of discussion was the table. Production asked engineering why they didn't design a table that required less production time, less welding, and was stronger. Engineering was offended in that they claimed that they designed the best table possible. Production drew the table in Chart 8.1b where the entire structure was cut out of one piece of sheet metal and challenged engineering to prove that their version was better. With this example, and others like it, engineering realized that they needed to work closely with production and that production knew best how to "produce." A new team-based engineering design approach was introduced into the organization which broke down the silos. Is this an example that can also be applied to the Architectural, Engineering, and Construction (AEC) industry? Are there times when construction should be consulted and that working together with the subcontractors can actually add value to the end product?

Establishing a direction is all about influencing and managing change. Organizations will often resist change and will attempt to persist in their comfort zone. However, change will happen whether you resist it or embrace it. The ideal approach is to develop an organization that drives

(a)   (b)

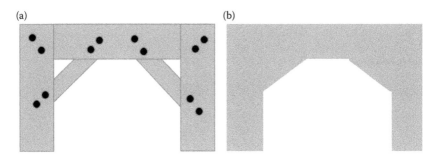

CHART 8.1
Table example.

innovative progress and leaves the comfort zone behind. This type of organization will be able to break through the complacency and lack of awareness that the comfort zone breeds and move forward into a highly competitive position conducive to long-lasting success.

> Leadership is about setting a direction. It's about creating a vision, empowering and inspiring people to want to achieve the vision, and enabling them to do so with energy and speed through an effective strategy. In its most basic sense, leadership is about mobilizing a group of people to jump into a better future.
>
> **John P. Kotter,**
> *Kotter International*

8.2 CORE COMPETENCIES

A core competency is a service or skill that the organization is exceptional at executing. It is what sets the organization apart from the competition. It is what stands out in the eyes of the client. Taking the time to clearly define the core competencies of the organization can create more confident and purpose-driven managers and staff and can help direct efforts to improve services and identify waste.

Initially, the purpose of defining the company's core competencies may not be clear. Many executives may think the company's core competencies are already obvious. However, if 10 members of the organization are asked what the company is great at, 10 different answers will most likely be provided. An organization that does not have a clear and common understanding of their core competencies will result in different managers dedicating improvement efforts that fit into their own personal perception of what the company should be great at. Unfortunately, this may not be aligned with the organization's true core competencies.

A core competency is not just what the members of the organization think they're good at. It is better defined as what the organization excels at. It is a service that your organization can provide better than anyone else. Core competencies should be made obvious to the members of the organization as well as to the client by clearly defining them. It's not what an organization is good at, it's what the organization is truly superior at.

Defining core competencies can provide direction for the organization. Managers will have a clear focus on what their staff are expected to excel at and marketers will have a common understanding of what sets the company apart. Additionally, focusing on core competencies can provide insight into what training and coaching opportunities are of highest value to the organization. Defining the organization's core competencies can also provide insight into which tasks may be better outsourced or completed by a partner or sub-consultant.

An organization that is focused on core competencies will be constantly looking for opportunities to become even better at what they are great at and the effective allocation of resources will become clear. The organization's professional expertise can become so clear that clients will know that there is no other source to turn to when they need the services that your organization provides. Through this, the company's competitive position will become solid.

8.3 VISION

The strategic vision is a clear, concise, forward-looking statement that establishes the desired future state of the organization and will act as a foundation for the entire strategic plan. Developing a vision for the organization is a team effort and is accomplished through a series of workshops. These workshops include key individuals at the top levels of the organization and consider insight and suggestions from employees at all levels.

Developing a strategic vision can take time. Don't rush it! Allow the time necessary to develop a vision that the entire organization will be excited to support. The vision will provide direction for important future decisions and will create a clear focus for the strategic planning process. The vision is for the employees. It should illustrate long-term perspective and stability that will inspire confidence and trust. It should establish a contagious sense of passion for the organization defining where it is going in such a way that it will attract and retain top talent. Think of it not only as a statement of the organization's vision but also the organization's passion.

When writing the vision, avoid buzzwords. Avoid using language that sounds generic. A generic vision will seem cheap and will fail to inspire employees to support it. Paint a picture of the future of the organization in a way that employees will be inspired and challenged to improve. Keep it concise and clear. The following questions should be discussed in visioning workshops to direct the development of the strategic vision.

- What does our organization do?
- What makes our organization unique?
- What makes our organization highly qualified?
- What makes our organization real (relatable)?

8.4 MISSION

The strategic mission statement is a description of the purpose of the organization and is developed to guide its actions and decision-making processes. While the vision statement can be thought of as what the organization will become, the mission statement can be thought of as what the organization will do to realize the vision. The mission statement provides a focused direction toward which the entire organization can direct its efforts. It provides an essential framework for decision making and sets a solid foundation for the firm's strategy.

An engineering firm without a clear united mission will likely divide itself into factions either by geographical region or by function. Each faction will have its own priorities and goals and will give little importance to the goals of the other factions. For example, two common factions may be the civil engineers and the structural engineers. A lack of mission may result in a civil group setting goals that are highly focused on quality while the structural group may set goals that are more focused on speed. As the two groups are required to work together, the civil group becomes frustrated with the structural group's lack of attention to detail while the structural group is frustrated with the civil group's lack of adherence to the schedule. An organization divided into factions or silos will result in frustration, bitterness, and eventually a culture of unengaged and unenthusiastic employees who avoid any sort of teaming situations.

Establishing a mission statement is similar to bending a reflective surface into a parabolic reflector which collects many parallel light rays and redirects them towards a single focal point. When the light is focused on a single point, it can produce a significant increase in heat which the individual light rays could never achieve alone. AEC firms are full of highly intelligent and motivated individuals who have the capacity to achieve great feats. When all of their energy is redirected towards a single mission or focal point, their individual capacities are significantly magnified.

The mission statement should describe what service the firm provides, who the service is for, and what makes the firm uniquely capable of providing the service. Use dynamic and inspiring language that will drive employees to action. The mission statement should be short but packed with meaning and should convey a memorable message to clients.

8.5 DEFINING THE CUSTOMER

At your next project team meeting, ask those in attendance who the customer is. At your next executive meeting, ask those in attendance to define what is most important to the customer. You will find that many different answers will be provided. Everyone will have his/her own idea of who the client is and what is most important to that individual. Then, to take this exercise even further, ask your clients what they consider to be most important to them. In most cases, the answers you receive from the clients about what matters most will differ significantly from the answers you received from members of your organization.

Providing the service that the client wants is critical, and yet, most organizations do not fully understand the client's expectations and concerns. For this reason, defining the client is a very powerful aspect of the strategic planning process. Simply understanding what is most important to the client and building your business around the client's needs can set an organization apart from all of its competitors.

Take time to develop a common understanding of who the client is. Clearly define what is most important to the client and why. Develop an understanding of common pain points for the customer. Always involve the customer in this process. Ask questions and let the customer know you're working to design your strategy around his/her needs. Develop a systematic customer relationship management plan that will track and guide the efforts of the organization to develop and nurture long-lasting relationships.

Throughout the strategic planning process, refer to your definition of the customer. A customer-centric perspective will help to eliminate process complexities that do not add value to the customer. Business metrics will become more aligned with customer expectations and a customer-focused culture will prevail.

8.6 STRATEGIC PERSPECTIVES

Developing an effective strategy that will be applicable to everyone in the organization means that all perspectives should be incorporated into the plan. All of the different perspectives should be integrated into the development of strategic objectives and business metrics. This will ensure that the strategic plan is applicable to all departments throughout the organization. Additionally, involving departments with different perspectives in the strategic planning process will generate buy-in and ownership of the strategic plan. The four common perspectives that should be considered throughout the strategic planning process are financial, operational, employee based, and customer based.

8.6.1 Financial Perspective

Dr. Gerhard Plenert, a co-author of this book, was involved in the relocation of a transmission production plant from Jackson, Michigan to Queretaro, Mexico. The objective was to take advantage of the labor cost reduction that the company expected to get from the cheaper Mexican labor. Looking at the financial Key Performance Indicators (KPIs), the move was a success. The cost of operating the plant was significantly less than the cost of operating the previous plant in Michigan. However, the following KPI considerations were not considered:

1. The cost of transporting materials back and forth from Michigan to Mexico was allocated to overhead, not to the cost of operating the new facility.

2. The cost of the in-process transit inventory, which previously was a few days, was now measured in weeks and that cost was also allocated to overhead.
3. The total manufacturing lead time for the finished vehicle had increased because of the transport time.
4. Occasional border delays also increased the lead time.
5. One of the brass gears in the transmission had to be cut extremely precisely, and the machining in Mexico did not meet the required specs, thereby causing a large amount of waste. The decision was made to have the gear produced in Japan and then transported to Mexico to be installed into the transmission. These costs were allocated to overhead.

The financial KPIs said that moving the plant was a smart move. But if all the overhead that was specific to the new location was added back to the Mexico plant, the cost of the new facility was higher than the cost of the old facility in Michigan. The message is simple: "Don't trust the financial KPIs without looking at the big picture."

The financial perspective is typically the perspective that is at the forefront of most people's minds when they think of strategic planning. It is the perspective that is focused on the bottom line of the organization. The priorities of the financial perspective typically concentrate on increasing revenues and minimizing costs. This perspective may have objectives that revolve around creating growth, improving production efficiencies, and reducing unnecessary spending. The financial perspective should focus on long-term financial success and not just short-term fixes.

8.6.2 Operational Perspective

The operational perspective is focused on how things are getting done. How are projects being completed? The operational perspective is concerned with ensuring that staff members have available the resources necessary when they need them to get the job done on time. It also is concerned with ensuring that services are provided with a high level of quality and in the most efficient manner possible. Operations works to reduce unnecessary complexity and improve the agility of the company as it works to meet demanding schedules and shifting deadlines. Operational objectives will focus on reducing waste and continuously improving how things are getting done.

8.6.3 Employee-Based Perspective

The employee-based perspective is focused on maintaining a high level of employee engagement and attracting and retaining top talent. The employee perspective will revolve around the personal development of all members of the organization. Objectives will place high importance on employee satisfaction and the development and maintenance of a healthy organizational culture. Employee-based metrics will be primarily focused on promoting ideal, principle-based behaviors and successfully engaging staff and recognizing their value. The employee perspective will develop a culture that embraces the employees as the most valued asset of the organization and will work to develop their full potential.

8.6.4 Customer-Based Perspective

The customer-based perspective is primarily focused on the customer experience. It revolves around the needs, concerns, and expectations of the customer. The customer-based perspective will develop objectives that enhance the customer experience and turn customers into powerful evangelists of the organization. Priorities will focus on customer satisfaction and on generating new clients on a referral basis as opposed to cold calls. The customer-based perspective will work to generate a customer-centric organization.

8.7 PRIORITIES

The strategic mission will highlight several different priorities for the organization. These priorities will often require multiple objectives and a variety of business metrics to define and track performance from the points of view of the various strategic perspectives. At this point, the different corporate priorities should be listed and defined to help guide the development of objectives and metrics.

Create a clear and concise priority statement that outlines what the priority is. Then, create a clear and concise end-state statement that creates a mental image of what the successful achievement of this priority will look like. The end-state statement will help to guide the development of effective strategic objectives. Add a goal statement that provides a measurable benchmark that will guide the development of business metrics.

The use of strategic priorities is a powerful planning tool that will work to align objectives and metrics with the strategic mission of the organization. Aligning all aspects of the strategy with a common mission is one of the primary aspects of the strategic planning process and, if done effectively, will have a dramatic impact on the successful execution of the strategy.

8.8 SUMMARY

Establishing a direction is when you and your organization apply visionary thinking. It's an opportunity for you to escape the common approach to the strategy of trying to catch up to your competition. In the book, *Blue Ocean Strategy*, we read that "the only way to beat the competition is to stop trying to beat the competition" (Kim, Moauborgne, 2016). If you're constantly trying to catch up to the competition, then the best you'll ever do is catch up. Applying visionary thinking to your strategy requires a new way of thinking. In the book *Toyota's Global Marketing Strategy*, we learn that "in order to have thinking habits that are free from copy-catting, it is critical to establish a thinking habit that approaches everything starting with its essence and with the basics" (Hibino, Noguchi, Plenert, 2018). As you work to develop a direction for your organization, remember to start with the essence of what makes the organization valuable and the basics of what it aims to achieve. Focus on a unique direction that will drive your organization to a strategic position that will set it apart from the competition, rather than simply making it competitive.

9

Objectives

9.1 INTRODUCTION

Several years ago, Dr. Gerhard Plenert was involved in a project for the Texas Office of the Attorney General. This required working with 80 branch offices throughout the state and analyzing their performance. The environment was somewhat unique in that each office had two bosses, an office manager, and a lead attorney. Dr. Plenert would go to the offices one at a time and spend time there, analyzing flow, efficiencies, line balancing, employee satisfaction and participation, etc. Afterwards, he would sit down with the two "bosses" and give them a report on the performance of their branch along with recommendations. He discovered things like backlog of mail in someone's drawer that would exceed 1 year, work overlaps between employees, and major redundancies.

The results were mixed. Some locations paid attention to the recommendations and implemented changes. Others ignored the recommendations, feeling that they were either too busy to be bothered, or that they didn't feel the recommendations had merit. Because of the mixed level of interest, the reports received about any performance changes were also mixed. One of the Dallas offices excitedly called Dr. Plenert 2 weeks after his visit. They congratulated him and informed him that they had immediately implemented all his recommendations, and in two weeks, they had tripled their throughput. Is this an anomaly? Not really. Some organizations were receptive and interested in achieving excellence, and others were happy sitting where they were, not wanting to be part of the strategic objectives that the head office was striving towards.

Strategic objectives are long-term organization-wide goals that support the strategic mission and vision. Objectives capitalize on the core competencies of the organization and respond to internal and external influences in order to drive the organization in the right direction. They take the strategic mission and put it into action by breaking it down into action-oriented initiatives.

9.2 COMMON MISTAKES

Because strategic objectives will guide the efforts of the organization, it is important to make them as effective as possible. Understanding of few general mistakes will help get you started in the right direction. We'll focus on four main mistakes: lack of strategic alignment, focusing too much on symptoms, ignoring the client, and forgetting what you're great at. Then, we'll dive into what makes an objective great.

9.2.1 Lack of Strategic Alignment

A lack of strategic alignment means that a specific objective is a good idea but not necessarily in line with the strategic mission and vision. This mistake is very common. As an organization completes internal and external analyses, it is common to find many issues that would be beneficial to resolve, and it will be tempting to create objectives to try to fix all of the problems at once. This leads to a long and overwhelming list of objectives that don't necessarily support what the organization is trying to achieve. When the objectives are not strategically aligned, members of the organization can become confused about where the organization is going and why all these objectives are important. Remember the principle that too many objectives, goals, or metrics are as good as none, simply because they become confusing and employees will align themselves to whatever they choose as opposed to what leadership is striving for. As an organization is led with a common vision, many of the things that were considered problems become less important because the organization is focused on moving in a different direction.

9.2.2 Focusing Too Much on Symptoms

Focusing too much on symptoms means that the objectives are designed to cover up the evidence of a problem but do not clearly address the problem itself. Focusing on symptoms may provide short-term relief but will fail to create a maintainable improvement because sooner or later the symptoms will recur in either the same or different locations. Until the underlying problem is resolved, the symptoms will continue to plague the organization. Taking the time to fully analyze and understand the problem will inspire objectives that will drive long-lasting advances.

9.2.3 Ignoring the Client

Paying attention to what the client wants may initially seem like common sense. However, in many organizations, the things that matter most to the client can end up getting lost in what the organization assumes matters most to the client. Organizations will often assume they have a good understanding of the client's expectations and concerns without actually asking the client. Working hard to achieve success in areas the client doesn't actually care about can be a waste of resources and drive the cost of services to a level the client isn't willing to pay. Taking the time to fully understand the client's priorities will help strategic objectives to drive performance and encourage behaviors that will be much more valuable to the client.

9.2.4 Forgetting What You're Great At

It is common for organizations to get overly focused on solving problems and forget to also improve and be innovative in the areas where there doesn't appear to be any obvious problems. Becoming better at what you're already great at can easily become overwhelmed by the effort to fix problems. Truly exceptional organizations have not risen to that level by being mediocre at everything but by being better than anybody else at what they're great at. Although dealing with issues is important, don't forget to include objectives that also focus on enhancing the organization's strengths. Building continuous improvement into the corporate strategy will help drive an organization to the top of the pack and keep it there.

9.3 CHARACTERISTICS OF A GOOD OBJECTIVE

Now that we've discussed a few things to avoid regarding objectives, let's explore a few characteristics of good objectives. Creating great objectives can be the difference between a strategy that just takes up room on a bookshelf and one that becomes an active driving force throughout the organization. Taking time to ensure your objectives are effective will pay off in the long run.

9.3.1 Aligned with Strategic Mission

Strategic alignment is when all the efforts and resources of an organization are focused on a common vision. It's when every goal and decision in every unit and at every level of the organization are working together to accomplish a common future state. Organizations that achieve strategic alignment will experience dramatic increases in effective execution of the strategy. A strategically aligned organization will accomplish far more than an organization whose units are not working together. Ultimately, a strategic plan, no matter how elegant, cannot be effectively executed without enterprise alignment.

> Enterprises enjoying the greatest benefits from their new performance management systems are much better at aligning their corporate, business unit, and support unit strategies, and this indicates that alignment, much like the synchronism achieved by a high-performance rowing crew, produces dramatic benefits. Understanding how to create alignment in organizations is a big deal, one capable of producing significant payoffs for all types of enterprises.
>
> **Kaplan, Norton, 2006**

At this point, you've worked hard to develop an inspiring vision and a powerful mission; so, make sure you use it. Objectives exist to support the mission, not just to complete a strategic planning template found on the Internet. The objectives and the mission should have very clear and obvious connections and there should be no question as to how each objective is driving the mission forward. If the mission and the objectives are not aligned, members of the organization will naturally favor one or the other. Any inconsistency in the corporate strategy will act as a fork in the road requiring staff and managers to decide which path to focus on. Developing a united effort requires a consistently aligned strategy from top to bottom.

Ultimately, the basic concept of alignment is to keep the big picture clearly in your mind as you work out the smaller details of the strategy. Every small detail of the strategy from top to bottom should have a clear and obvious impact on the shared vision of the organization, as expressed in the following manner:

You've got to think about big things while you're doing small things, so that all the small things go in the right direction.

Alvin Toffler

9.3.2 Clear and Specific

Objectives must be written using very clear and specific language and leaving no room for interpretation or misinterpretation. Avoid using general language or empty words, such as "make it better" and "work to improve". These are empty statements because they give no understanding of what is truly intended. What does it mean to "make it better"? How much better? How will you know if "better" is achieved? Objectives should always be written in such a way that they clarify the intent of the mission, not muddy it up.

As an example, consider a manager who asks his/her staff to improve the quality of their deliverables but gives no common definition of what quality looks like. How will the staff know if they've achieved an improvement in quality? If the manager asks the staff in a meeting a month later how they're doing on quality, they can all honestly say they're doing great, no matter how "good" the quality of their deliverables actually is. Without a clear understanding of what the objective is, no one will truly know whether the product quality has been achieved and whether the staff performed in the manner expected per management standards.

> The benefits of increasing clarity are significant. You introduce an enormous amount of ease and efficiency into your organization. You improve the quality of decisions being made and the speed at which you operate. You create enormous capacity for value-adding and value-enabling work when people are not pursuing clarification. These benefits are all possible in organizations that commit themselves to clarity.
>
> **Martin, 2012**

9.3.3 Inclusive

An inclusive list of objectives will make the strategic mission applicable to all perspectives and priorities throughout the organization. This means that every member of the organization will clearly understand how he or she is able to support the mission of the organization. What is their role in the big picture? This is often spelled out in the metrics utilized to measure performance. No individual should be left out of having a clear under-standing of how he or she fits into the big picture.

9.3.4 Customer Centric

A customer-centric objective is one that is designed to add value to the client. Designing objectives that are customer centric means that each objective has a clear connection to what matters most to the client. Objectives that do not add value to the client will over time drive the client farther away. As resources are spent turning the organization into some-thing that is not valuable to the client, the gap between the organization's accomplishments and the client's expectations will grow wider. If the organization exists to provide a service, make sure that the service being perfected is actually wanted. Ensure that it is clear how each objective is adding value to the client.

Creating objectives that improve the organization's ability to provide the services that matter most to the client may seem obvious. However, this is a concept that is often completely disregarded by so many organiza-tions. Organizations can easily fall into the trap of assuming they know what is most important to the client and they begin focusing on objectives based on those assumptions. But, how can you be sure that what you are focusing your efforts on to improve the organization is actually important from the client's perspective if you haven't taken the time to ask the client?

As an example, consider an engineering firm that performs forensic investigations and then submits a report of the findings to the client. The manager of the engineering office feels the client would appreciate reports with additional documentation and more explanation of the findings. The manager instructs the staff engineers to work to add more detail to the reports. As a result, the reports begin to take more time to complete and, thus, the firm's fees for forensic services begin to increase. However, the reports that are produced are highly detailed and contain many photos, details, dimensions, etc. The manager of the engineering office is pleased with the outcome and is certain that the client is very impressed with all the added detail. To the manager's surprise, the firm's most critical clients begin using other firms for forensic services. When the manager meets with the clients to find out why they've taken their business elsewhere, the clients all agree that the fees of the engineering firm have become too high and that the firm takes too long to complete the reports. When the manager explains that the increased fees and increased amount of time needed to complete the reports are due to the high-level detail added to the reports, the clients explain that they don't need that much detail. What matters most to the clients is that the reports are completed quickly, the fees are kept reasonable, and that the information contained in the reports is concise and to the point.

In this case, the engineering firm spent significant time and resources making considerable improvements; however, they were the wrong improvements. If the strategic objectives are not adding value in the eyes of the client, they are likely decreasing value, even if they appear to be good objectives. An effective strategy applies the voice of the client to determine the difference between what good objectives are and what the best objectives are.

9.3.5 Simple

Reducing complexity should be carefully considered throughout the strategic planning process. Overly complicated objectives will create confusion, frustration, miscommunication, and indifference. Simplicity will make the objectives more manageable, measurable, and meaningful. The best objective is most often the simplest.

> Any intelligent fool can make things bigger, more complex, and more violent. It takes a touch of genius – and a lot of courage to move in the opposite direction.
>
> **E. F. Schumacher**

9.3.6 Measurable

Strategic objectives will generate business metrics, which means that objectives must be measurable. An objective that cannot be measured should not be considered an objective but rather a wish, and the strategic plan is no place for a wish list. The list of objectives must have associated measurable outcomes to drive performance and influence ideal behaviors throughout the organization. If an objective is not measurable, it's not important and it will not produce the desired results.

9.3.7 Realistic

Effective objectives can have a dramatic impact on the direction of the organization. However, if they are not realistic, the staff and managers will recognize this and will begin to develop their own, more realistic, objectives. Realistic objectives means that they are attainable within the given time and with the given resources and support. If an organization is asked to achieve an objective but does not provide the necessary resources, training, and time to accomplish it, the staff will become frustrated and refrain from giving the objective a reasonable effort. To effectively motivate an organization towards accomplishing an objective, the objective must be realistic.

9.3.8 Nonconflicting

Organizations will often find themselves wanting to fix everything all at once. They will develop a long list of objectives, and as a result, many of those objectives will be conflicting. For example, an organization may develop an objective to drastically improve the quality of deliverables. The same organization may develop an objective to drastically improve the speed of deliverable production. The staff will be conflicted as to whether to focus on quality or speed. They will inevitably need to choose one or the other or ignore both objectives altogether. Improving an organization will typically occur through a series of steps, rather than in one fell swoop. Improvement through steps and continuous improvement can be more effective than trying to fix everything all at once and will help to reduce the need for conflicting objectives.

9.3.9 Challenging

In order for objectives to be truly powerful, they must be challenging. They must inspire the members of the organization to push themselves to new limits. Objectives must make it clear that the organization will not continue to operate as usual but will be taking major strides in a positive direction. Accomplishing an objective should result in a noticeable change, not just a minor heightening to the norm, as described in the following excerpt:

> Goals that start with phrases like 'Continue to…', 'Maintain our…' or 'Strive to' aren't really goals at all. They state the obvious, and say little more than 'We're going to keep going as we have been'. Strategy is about change, improvement and getting better results than we have gotten so far. We don't get better results by continuing to do the same things.

Barr, 2014

9.4 DEVELOPING OBJECTIVES

The development of strategic objectives should be conducted as a team to ensure that all perspectives and priorities are considered. The objectives should be focused on supporting the strategic mission. Begin the group discussion by establishing a shared understanding of what strategic objectives are and what they are for. Read through the strategic mission and break it down to ensure common understanding. Begin listing the objectives to drive the mission forward. Discuss the objectives from the point of view of various perspectives and priorities. Once a thorough list of potential objectives has been developed, begin thinking about how the objectives can be reduced, simplified, and clarified. Ensure that each objective will clearly add value to the customer and remember to focus on enhancing the strengths of the organization as well as correcting the issues. Go through the list of objectives and ensure each one fulfills the characteristics of a good objective, as previously discussed.

Going through the process of developing strategic objectives requires the group to work together. Avoid the temptation to develop objectives alone and then present them to the group for approval. The group discussion required to develop objectives is a valuable tool for developing objectives that will be meaningful to the entire organization. At times during the discussion, you may find it necessary to seek input from other individuals throughout the organization. Involving others will help build buy-in and ownership of the objectives developed. Don't rush the process. The process is just as important as the outcome.

9.5 SUMMARY

Establishing objectives is critical to the success of every enterprise. Objectives lead to executable actions that the individuals of the organization can take to support the corporate strategy. However, achieving an objective is not a true success if the guiding principles and values of the organization were compromised to achieve it. Ensure that the developed objectives will not encourage unethical behaviors within the organization. Every objective should be designed to not only achieve financial success but also enhance the positive culture of the organization and add value to the client. An organization that enhances the quality of life of its employees and customers will enjoy greater and longer-lasting success than an unethical organization ever will, as described in the following excerpt:

> The corporate value system needs to be at the heart of all goals and the implementation. Values should be incorporated into, not take a back seat to, goal achievement. For example, honesty and integrity are often thrown to the wind in order to make the numbers look good. A company that loses its values to numbers will have a long road back trying to recover its lost integrity. And, since the numbers weren't realistic anyway, the company will also have trouble achieving its "realistic" goals.
>
> **Plenert, 1995**

10

Metrics

10.1 INTRODUCTION

A famous international truck manufacturer (I'm not going to say the name but if you're familiar with the industry, you'll know who I'm talking about) was assessing their performance using performance metric Key Performance Indicators (KPIs). Each plant was evaluated and ranked based on their KPI performance. The assessment process included direct costs that could be connected directly with a plant and indirect corporate costs, which were allocated across all production facilities.

After reviewing the performance of all the plants, one of the plants was losing money in that their cost of operation (direct plus indirect costs) was greater than their revenue. The corporate decision was made to close the plant.

Closing the plant caused the indirect corporate costs to be now allocated across one fewer production facility. Corporate costs, of course, did not decrease with the closure of one of the plants. This, of course, meant that the operating costs (direct plus indirect) of each plant were now higher. Guess what? Another one of the production facilities, which previously was barely in the black, now found itself in the red. The decision was made to close the facility.

This process of allocating costs and closing plants continued until eventually, the manufacturer was on the verge of bankruptcy and ended up being bought out. For us on the outside, this seems ridiculously stupid. But when viewed from the inside, where the leadership couldn't see the forest for the trees, it all seemed logical.

Business metrics seem to be one of those areas of a business strategy that organizations dread, avoid, and ignore more than any other. Yet, the creation and use of effective metrics are one of the most important elements of bringing a strategy to life. The effective creation and use of metrics can be the difference between a business strategy that sits on a shelf collecting dust and one where an organization realizes its vision.

Many of the concerns that members of organizations have regarding metrics have arisen over years of dealing with ineffective and, at times, harmful business metrics. In this chapter, we'll discuss the purpose of metrics and several of the most common mistakes organizations make with metrics. We'll also discuss the recommended process for creating business metrics and how this process will assist in overcoming many of the mistakes and challenges associated with metrics.

10.2 UNDERSTANDING THE PURPOSE OF METRICS

Business metrics are measurements that track progressive changes in various business processes over time. The use of metrics creates a united team effort and transforms a written strategy into a living strategy. Metrics also create opportunities for employees to observe the results of their efforts which can help develop ownership of strategic objectives. Establishing and utilizing metrics are critical to the success of any strategy. However, selecting the wrong metrics can be counterproductive and possibly detrimental to the organization. Likewise, creating a strategy without measuring how it affects the organization can create indifference to the strategy.

Much of the animosity and anxiety that exists within organizations regarding metrics is due to a misunderstanding of what metrics are for. The purpose of establishing and tracking metrics is simply to motivate performance and influence behaviors. When organizations use them to do more than this, they become detrimental and overbearing.

Metrics motivate performance by focusing the attention of the organization on what the strategy is intended to achieve. Team leaders and team members develop a united effort to move the performance needle in the right direction. The metrics become a common and constant source of motivation to achieve strategic objectives. A business metric that is specifically designed to motivate performance will be referred to in this book as a KPI.

Metrics influence behavior by establishing a clear understating of what the organization considers to be "good behavior." Too often, a cancer of bad behavior can spread throughout an organization simply because clear expectations have not been established. Establishing metrics can help to define and guide good behaviors and prevent bad behaviors. A business metric that is specifically designed to influence behavior will be referred to in this book as a Key Behavior Indicator (KBI).

KPIs and KBIs are both critical for the successful establishment and implementation of business metrics. KPIs without KBIs may produce high short-term performance, but that performance will be unsustainable and possibly detrimental in ways the organization didn't anticipate. Driving performance by influencing good behaviors (KPIs with KBIs) can produce high long-term performance and will benefit the organization and its clients in many other positive ways.

10.3 KPIs vs. KBIs

A business metric that is intended to drive performance in an organization is typically referred to as KPI. KPIs are used on a regular basis and most managers throughout the Architectural, Engineering, and Construction (AEC) industry are familiar with the term. A less familiar term is KBI. KBIs are business metrics that are intended to influence behaviors. Because the purpose of measuring is to drive performance and influence behaviors, both KPIs and KBIs are essential metrics to a business strategy.

The purpose of using KPIs is to measure the performance areas that need to be driven. Any aspect of the organization's current performance that needs to be improved must be measured. Performance is highly unlikely to change in the intended ways unless it is measured. Developing KPIs creates well-defined performance targets for the entire organization to focus on.

So, if KPIs are driving performance, why does an organization need KBIs? Because KPIs are lagging indicators, which means that they report what has happened in the past and give minimal direction for the future. KBIs are leading indicators, which means they are forward-looking and predictive. By following KBIs, we are still able to shift direction, when necessary, before the KPIs are cemented in. KPIs are instructive both inside and outside the organization because they are an indicator of the successful performance of the organization. They tell everyone if we have been successful. We gave the example earlier of how many toilets should be manufactured. Should we look at KPIs like last year's sales, or should we look at KBIs like the number of housing starts?

Additionally, we use both KPIs and KBIs because performance is heavily influenced by behavior. Positive behaviors can improve performance and then maintain high performance. Negative behaviors can prevent higher performance standards from being achieved. In essence, it's the change in behavior that ultimately creates a lasting change in performance.

Too often, organizations create a long list of KPIs that are meaningless to the staff-level members of the organization because the staff members do not have a clear understating of how they can affect the high-level KPIs. For example, the corporate strategy may include a KPI having to do with increasing the profit margin. However, a staff engineer is focused on simply completing the tasks assigned to him or her and may not see how the KPI is affected by his or her daily tasks. But, when a KBI associated with speeding up project turnaround time is established that supports the KPI for increasing the company's profit margin, it becomes clear how the staff members can support the corporate strategy.

Typically, KPIs are more meaningful to executives and KBIs are more meaningful to staff members. In a quarterly executive meeting, it would mostly be the KPIs that are discussed. In a weekly staff meeting, it would most likely be the KBIs that are discussed. For this reason, the KBIs must support the KPIs, which, in turn, support the corporate objectives. By aligning metrics in this way, members of the organization at all levels can understand their role in supporting the corporate strategy.

KPIs and KBIs are not the same for every organization. They are unique and customized to the corporate strategy and will change over time as the strategic objectives change. Later in this chapter, the process for developing metrics is discussed. Several examples of KPIs and KBIs are listed. However, it should be clearly understood that no organization should simply pick a few common metrics and put them into practice. The process of developing customized metrics is just as important as the resulting metrics and their applications. The following lists are only a few common examples and are simply meant to seed your organization's development of its own metrics.

10.4 EXAMPLES OF KPIs

10.4.1 Backlog Volume

The backlog volume is the amount of accumulated work in the queue waiting to be completed. Maintaining a healthy backlog volume is critical to the future success of every firm. Keeping track of the firm's backlog volume can help identify lean seasons, identify potential trends, and predict future staffing needs.

10.4.2 Break-Even Point

The break-even point is the amount of revenue for a given period of time that needs to be collected in order to cover all the expenses for the same period of time. It's the point at which revenue is equal to expenses. The goal, of course, is to produce enough revenue to exceed the break-even point in order to be left with a profit. Keeping track of the revenue and how close you are to the break-even point can help determine clear revenue goals for a specified time period.

10.4.3 Utilization Rate

The utilization rate is the percentage of time spent working on billable projects in comparison to the total hours worked. It's common for the production staff to have a utilization rate of 70%–85% while a manager may have a utilization rate of around 60%–70%. The utilization rate is calculated as follows:

$$\text{Utilization Rate} = \frac{\text{Billable Time}}{\text{Total Time}}$$

10.4.4 Client Satisfaction

Client satisfaction is typically determined using client surveys, which can be conducted continuously or at set intervals of time. A client satisfaction survey typically consists of a series of questions that produce quantifiable responses. Quantifiable responses may consist of yes or no or a selection from a range of numbers, such as 0–10. An example of a question that produces a quantifiable response may be "in a range of 0 to 10, how satisfied are you with the firm's responsiveness." These types of quantifiable responses can be tracked over time and graphed to provide a visual display of the firm's progress towards a client satisfaction goal.

10.4.5 Net Promoter Score

Net Promoter Score (NPS) is used to determine how likely current clients are to promote the organization. It involves asking current clients, "On a scale of 0 to 10, how likely are you to recommend our firm's services to a valued colleague?" Responses ranging from 0 to 6 are considered "Detractors," which are the individuals who would be most likely to tell a valued colleague not to use your firm. Responses ranging from 7 to 8 are considered "Passives," which are the individuals who would not recommend your firm to a valued colleague but would also not tell them not to use your firm. Responses ranging from 9 to 10 are considered "Promoters," which are the individuals who would recommend your firm to a valued colleague. The net promoter score is then calculated as follows:

$$NPS = \frac{(\# \text{ of Promoters}) - (\# \text{ of Detractors})}{\text{Total} \# \text{ of Respondents}} \times 100$$

A high NPS suggests that those surveyed are "evangelists" for your firm or that they are likely to actively promote your services to others. A firm with a high NPS will be likely to obtain a significant number of new clients by referrals.

10.4.6 Client Lifetime Value

The Client Lifetime Value (CLV) is the total amount of revenue predicted to be collected over the lifetime of the organization's relationship with a specific client. The CLV is typically calculated using historical revenue data projected into the future. Using trends generated by analyzing the historical revenue data can identify trends and possible causes for increases and decreases in revenue. The CLV can provide insight into how many resources should be dedicated to obtaining specific types of clients and which types of clients have the greatest value to the organization. The CLV can also help to clarify the benefits of dedicating resources to the retention of specific types of clients. Although the CLV is a prediction, it can help to direct marketing and business development efforts towards the most valuable clients and prevent dedication of excessive resources on less valuable clients.

10.4.7 Actual Revenue vs. Projected Revenue

The ratio of actual revenue to projected revenue provides insight into the organization's ability to meet projections. This information can help direct future efforts and identify potential needs for changes to the organization's strategic planning and management efforts.

10.4.8 Actual Cost vs. Projected Cost

The ratio of actual cost to projected cost provides insight into the organization's ability to keep costs at or below the projected levels. Measuring this type of data can help the management team identify unexpected and possibly avoidable costs to the organization.

10.4.9 Profit

The need to measure the profits produced by an organization seems obvious. However, the benefits that result from the measurements can at times be overlooked and undervalued. Measuring profits on a regular basis can help identify trends and potential issues when they are young. Identifying potential issues early can help to identify opportunities for improvement. When issues with profitability are not identified until they have fully matured, this situation can be detrimental and potentially disastrous to the organization. Additionally, simply keeping a constant eye on profitability can help provide common ground for various departments of the organization to build on, thus helping to create a united effort.

10.4.10 Cost

The need to keep track of costs is obvious. However, measuring and monitoring costs can help provide insight into trends. Recognizing trends can help the organization plan for times when expenses are typically high.

10.4.11 Client Acquisition Cost

The Client Acquisition Cost (CAC) is the amount of money spent by a firm to activate a new client. The CAC is calculated by dividing the sum of the costs spent on obtaining new clients by the number of new clients obtained. The CAC can provide insight into the effectiveness of executed marketing strategies and campaigns.

10.4.12 Project Acquisition Cost

The Project Acquisition Cost (PAC) is the amount of money spent by a firm to obtain a new project. The PAC is calculated by dividing the sum of the costs spent on obtaining new projects by the number of projects obtained. The PAC can provide insight into the effectiveness of the firm's efforts to obtain new projects. It may also influence what types of projects are the most profitable for the organization.

10.4.13 Number of Proposals Written

Keeping track of the number of proposals written can provide insight into possible proposal writing trends and deficiencies. Times of a light workload can often be traced back to times when insufficient resources were dedicated to writing proposals. When the workload is heavy, proposal writing tends to slow, which can lead to a light workload in the future. Setting proposal writing goals can help maintain constant attention on pursuing new projects, which may help reduce fluctuations in workload.

10.4.14 Employee Satisfaction

Employee satisfaction is critical to achieving strategic performance objectives. However, measuring employee satisfaction accurately can often be a significant challenge. Common ways to measure employee satisfaction is by using suggestion boxes, anonymous employee surveys, and employee reviews. The types of questions asked in surveys and reviews should produce measurable responses that can be tracked over time to determine if improvement is being made. It is also critical that employees see positive changes happening as a result of their willingness to express their satisfaction or dissatisfaction. If the employee's sharing of his or her concerns has no effect, the employee may become indifferent towards the suggestion boxes, surveys, and reviews.

Employee satisfaction can also be researched using external sources, such as online employee recruiting websites. Such websites often collect employee satisfaction information from current and previous employees. By reviewing what previous employees are saying about the firm through external sources, management can learn about issues that current employees may be too afraid to discuss.

10.4.15 Employee Engagement

Employee engagement goes beyond employee satisfaction in that it indicates a sense of commitment to the firm and not just satisfaction in working there. One common way to measure employee engagement is the Employee Net Promoter Score (ENPS), which is used to determine how likely current employees would be to recommend employment with the organization to a close friend or family member. It involves asking current employees, "On a scale of 0 to 10, how likely would you be to recommend employment with our firm to a close friend or loved one?" Responses ranging from 0 to 6 are considered "Detractors," which are the employees who would be most likely to tell a close friend or loved one not to work at your firm. Responses ranging from 7 to 8 are considered "Passives," which are the employees who would not recommend employment with the firm to a close friend or loved one but would also not tell them not to work at the firm. Responses ranging from 9 to 10 are considered "Promoters," which are the employees that would recommend employment with the firm to a close friend or loved one. The net promoter score is then calculated as follows:

$$\text{ENPS} = \frac{\left(\text{\# of Promoters}\right) - \left(\text{\# of Detractors}\right)}{\text{Total \# of Respondents}} \times 100$$

A high ENPS suggests that those surveyed are highly engaged and are committed to the firm or that they are likely to actively promote employment with the firm.

10.4.16 Employee Turnover Rate

The employee turnover rate is a ratio of the total number of voluntary and involuntary separations with respect to the total number of employees. Keeping the employee turnover rate low indicates that the organization is doing a good job of retaining employees. Retaining employees can help maintain high morale within the company and can demonstrate stability to clients. A low turnover rate can also reduce new employee training costs and make the services provided to customers more consistent and reliable.

10.4.17 Revenue per Billable Employee

Revenue per billable employee is the ratio of total revenue to the number of billable employees. Tracking the revenue per billable employee can provide insight into the overall productivity of the workforce.

10.4.18 Project Overrun

The project overrun is the amount of costs that exceed the project budget. Tracking project overruns can provide insight into the production efficiency of the firm's operations. Analyzing project overruns can also help a firm identify the types of projects or services for which the firm may not be charging enough to make a profit.

10.4.19 Overhead

Overhead is the indirect costs associated with doing business. Keeping track of overhead for regular time periods can provide insight into highs and lows as well as abnormal conditions. As businesses look for opportunities to reduce waste in their operations, they will become more competitive and profitable.

10.4.20 Number of New Clients

At times, organizations can become comfortable with their existing client pool and overlook the need to work to attract new clients. This type of complacency can often result in a downturn in opportunities in the future. Keeping track of the number of new clients acquired for a regular time period can help keep the focus on marketing efforts.

10.4.21 Number of New Clients by Referral

Obtaining new clients is always important. However, how those new clients are obtained is also very important. One great way to develop long-lasting relationships is to make sure your current clients are so satisfied with your service that they refer their associates to you. This results in new clients who already have positive feelings towards your organization. Keeping track of the number of clients acquired by referral will help to focus marketing and business development efforts in such a way that current clients will not be neglected and new clients will be excited to develop the new relationship with your organization.

10.4.22 Hit Rate

The hit rate is the percentage of proposals won to the total number of proposals written. Writing proposals can be a time-consuming process and it is in the best interest of the organization to work to maintain a high hit rate. Keeping track of the hit rate can focus the efforts of those writing proposals in such a way that the goal will be to win the projects and not just complete the task of writing the proposal.

10.5 EXAMPLES OF KBIS

10.5.1 Suggestions

Creating an opportunity for all members of the organization to make suggestions helps to build a more engaged workforce. Suggestions should be encouraged and implemented as appropriate in a timely manner. Keeping track of the number of suggestions provided in a regular amount of time can help an organization keep track of the participation rate. Implementing strategically aligned suggestions can build a culture where all employees know that they have a voice in the improvements made to the organization.

10.5.2 Collaboration

It is common for silos to exist throughout organizations in the AEC industry. Silos are task-oriented teams that tend to operate independently and tend to take little to no thought regarding how their efforts will affect other teams in the organization. This type of mind-set can produce an unhealthy competitive culture in which teams focus only on their own successes and are indifferent to the success of the organization as a whole. Observing the level of trust between teams can help build a culture of collaboration and overcome some of the frustrations and efficiency losses that can occur from a lack of synergistic cooperation. Employee surveys or regular observations can be effective ways to measure levels of collaboration as well as track the effectiveness of team building activities.

10.5.3 Recognition

Maintaining a well-motivated workforce is a common challenge within every organization. Although motivation can be generated through many means, one common method is to recognize successes. Recognition should happen on a regular basis and should be consistent and highly evident to promote a recurrence of the successes being recognized.

10.5.4 Onboarding

Organizations should use a comprehensive onboarding process to provide necessary training, cultural initiation, and familiarization with the organization's standard processes. The onboarding process can also be an effective way to reinforce the energy brought into the organization by excited new hires. The onboarding process should be continuously improved by observing the effectiveness of existing efforts.

10.5.5 Challenging Current Processes

Many organizations miss great opportunities to improve their processes because of a tendency to keep doing things the way they've always been done. Exceptional ideas for improvements can often come from the production staff who must address the challenges of the current processes on a daily basis. Organizations should have a regular and effective approach towards challenging the current processes.

10.5.6 Positive Approach to Failures

Failures are typically perceived as events that require harsh chastening and occasionally demotions or layoffs. This approach fails to take advantage of an opportunity to recognize the flaws in the system that led to the failure in the first place. Failures should be approached with a positive attitude to improve operations and learn from the failures. Failures can also trigger action items or special projects that can result in significant improvements to the organization.

10.5.7 Problem-Solving Training

Problems will always come up and will arise at all levels of the organization. Unfortunately, many problems are never resolved because those enduring the problems do not know how to resolve them or do not feel empowered to resolve them. Too often, they are caught up in tradition, which says, "We've always done it that way," or they don't realize that there is an alternative way of approaching the problem. Training all employees to solve problems as they occur can result in improvements at all levels of the organization. Problem-solving techniques, like Lean or Six Sigma techniques, should be scientific and supported by regular coaching by leadership. Effective training and coaching will make the recurrence of problems a less common event. Each member of the organization should also have a clear understanding of his or her authority to solve problems.

10.5.8 Systems Approach

Using a systems approach to problems means that as issues come up, an analysis of the system is conducted instead of searching for an individual to blame. Negative behaviors in organizations are often unknowingly encouraged by system flaws. As problems are analyzed, the temptation to place blame should be avoided. It can be helpful to avoid using names and personal reasons for process failures. Analyzing the system for causes of the problem, instead of placing blame on individuals, can help maintain a positive culture and can prevent the system from encouraging further negative behaviors.

10.5.9 Visual Operations Management

As work flows through the organization, it can be common for the members of the organization to become lost in their individual task and lose sight of the overall flow of the work. Creating visual presentations of the flow of work will make it easy to see the conditions of operations in real time. Additionally, real-time visual presentations of the flow of work will make any abnormal conditions obvious, resulting in a quick response to undesirable situations.

10.5.10 Effective Scheduling

Effective scheduling will provide a more consistent workload and help to alleviate the "feast or famine" that exists in so many organizations within the AEC industry. Production should be directly linked to customer demands and delivery expectations. Upcoming work should be highly visible to provide sufficient opportunities to plan for resource needs and irregular fluctuations in customer expectations.

10.5.11 Bottlenecks

Bottlenecks are common in any operation but too often they are perceived as unavoidable and unmanageable, and as a result, the negative impact of bottlenecks are rarely relieved. Organizations that recognize their operational bottlenecks and measure their impact will be more likely to identify opportunities to improve the situation. Read the book, *The Goal*, by Eli Goldratt if you are interested in resolving bottlenecks within your organization.

10.5.12 Firefighting

Many organizations become accustomed to fighting fires, and as a result, they miss out on opportunities to improve their operations because their focus is on the fires. Recognizing and measuring the impact of firefighting events can make it more obvious how to prevent them in the future, thus providing more opportunities to develop lasting improvements.

In our consulting work with organizations worldwide, we have determined that there are basically two types of organizations: (1) those that are looking to improve and (2) those that are too busy fighting fires to worry about getting better. Which one are you?

10.5.13 Customer Focus

The expectations of the customer should be clearly understood, and each member of the organization should have an understanding of how his or her efforts create value for the customer. Regular feedback from customers should be utilized quickly and sufficient time should be taken to understand what services are considered the most valuable to the client and which are perceived as unnecessary.

10.6 COMMON MISTAKES AND APPREHENSIONS

Organizations often have common apprehensions about business metrics, many of which are justified due to earlier bad experiences with ineffective and detrimental metrics. Understanding some of the most common apprehensions and mistakes that organizations experience can help team leaders overcome them. Here we will discuss some of the most common mistakes and apprehensions in order to build awareness. The approach to creating metrics discussed later in this chapter will help overcome these apprehensions and prevent mistakes.

10.6.1 Creating Too Much Work

As organizations begin working to develop strategic objectives and goals, leaders can often have a desire to fix all the problems within their organization. Instead of focusing on just a few of the issues at a time, they try to fix them all at once. This approach results in a multitude of metrics that require managers and staff members to spend much of their time recording and reporting data. Too many metrics can result in too much work collecting data and can cause a reduction in performance simply because of the increased workload caused by the metrics. Remove yourself from the false assumption that "all data are good data."

10.6.2 Lack of Buy-In

A lack of buy-in occurs when metrics are selected and are imposed on managers and staff members who were not involved in the metrics creation process. If buy-in is not established among those responsible for collecting and reporting data, indifference towards the metrics and associated data collection and reporting processes will result. Additionally, a lack of buy-in can result in misunderstandings about what the metrics are for, why they're important, and how they'll be used.

10.6.3 Gaming the System

Gaming the system refers to the intentional manipulation of the data to make the reports look more respectable. Knowing the numbers can be and often are manipulated results in a general distrust of the data. Managers can spend hours arguing over whether the data are accurate enough to make important decisions based on the data. It is often common for the management team to point fingers at staff for gaming the system. However, the truth is that gaming the system is usually the result of poor metrics and the poor implementation of metrics.

Gaming the system is extremely common at all levels of the organization. Even the numbers that the CEO reports to the Board of Directors are often tweaked. That is why it is critical that the metrics that we select are aimed at our strategic priorities. It keeps the focus where it correctly belongs.

10.6.4 Using Measures to Punish

Unfortunately, managers will often use the results of the data to punish or even lay off staff members. Using metrics to punish creates animosity towards the system and a culture of fear and disloyalty. Manipulation of the numbers and a feeling of tension within the team will always result.

Staff members will often use the numbers to focus blame on others in an attempt to protect their own jobs. Metrics are a tool used to motivate performance and influence behavior. They are not meant to be a source of fear and animosity but a source of positive inspiration.

10.7 CHARACTERISTICS OF A GOOD METRIC

Now that we've developed an understanding of what not to do with metrics, let's take a minute to discuss a few of the characteristics of a good metric. Good metrics don't happen by accident nor do they happen simply by measuring what everyone else seems to be measuring. Every organization is different and requires a customized set of measures to effectively drive performance and influence behaviors. Truly productive metrics are uniquely and carefully designed to meet the needs of the organization.

10.7.1 Feasible

A feasible metric should be relatively simple to measure. An overly complicated metric that requires excessive data collection will result in an unnecessary increase in workload. To help keep metrics feasible, focus on the purpose of the metric. Consider the performance that is intended to be improved and determine the simplest way to track it. Consider the behavior that is intended to be influenced and determine if there is a simpler way to observe it. Keeping metrics feasible will not only result in a lighter workload but also an increase in buy-in from those responsible for tracking the data.

10.7.2 Controllable

A controllable metric is one that can be directly influenced by those responsible for its improvement. When employees are responsible for metrics that they cannot influence, direct, or regulate, they become frustrated and lose interest in supporting the metric. In many cases, the influence that lower-level staff members have on KPIs is not immediately apparent. The metrics team should take this into consideration as they define metrics to ensure that each member of the organization has a clear understanding of how to support the metrics. The use of KBIs is a great way to provide each team with clear insight into how their actions can move the performance needle in the right direction.

10.7.3 Focused on the Future

An organization that focuses too much on what other organizations are already doing will always be doing nothing more than trying to catch up. Truly innovative organizations maintain a focus on the future. It's for this reason that a strategic plan should start with a clear and inspiring vision of what the organization is meant to become. That vision then guides the rest of the strategic plan, including the strategic metrics. As the metrics team works to develop strategic metrics, consider whether the metrics being developed will drive performance that will ultimately result in the realization of that inspired vision. Metrics that are only focused on catching up to other organizations or even maintaining current levels of performance will never result in truly innovative change.

10.7.4 Clear

A clear metric is one that has been carefully designed to avoid confusion or misinterpretation. When a metric is clear, it is easy for users to understand how to collect data and what the data will be used for. It is also easy to identify how the metrics will drive performance and influence behavior in a way that works towards achieving strategic objectives. Without clarity, metrics may produce unintended results and the collected data may not be as reliable as desired because the staff members misunderstand what the measures are for. A great way to make metrics clear is to take the time to fully define them. The process of fully defining metrics will be discussed later in this chapter.

10.7.5 Specific

A specific metric is one that is strategically focused and precisely defined, rather than broad reaching and general. Metrics lacking in specificity often result in a lack of focused direction. Much of the energy exerted in supporting the metrics can be misdirected and as a result, wasted. Additionally, members of the organization can end up working against each other because nonspecific metrics do not provide a sufficiently focused effort. Specific results require specific metrics.

10.7.6 Logical

A logical metric is one that makes sense to users and seems to be a natural or sensible choice given the strategic objectives. Although creativity is beneficial and even necessary during the metrics development process, that creativity should remain married to a clear logic. Producing metrics that seem illogical or nonsensical can make it very difficult to encourage enterprise-wide buy-in and ownership of those metrics. If members of the organization cannot understand the logic of the metrics, they will often look for logic by creating their own metrics, which may result in counterproductive behaviors. Logical metrics produce a general sense of understating and increase ownership of the metrics throughout the organization because they follow a natural choice.

10.8 HOW TO SELECT APPROPRIATE METRICS

Most organizations have several business metrics, and employees are instructed on which numbers to keep track of. In general, it is understood that tracking performance data is important. However, not all data are good data and not every metric selection process produces productive metrics. In fact, the process of selecting metrics can at times create indifference and even hostility towards the metrics and the team that selected them. In this section, we discuss an effective process of developing metrics.

Selecting appropriate metrics requires more than just a brainstorming session where a few common metrics are selected. It takes more than just selecting a few of the convenient measures already being produced by the organization's existing accounting and staffing software. The ideal approach to selecting metrics requires beginning with the end in mind, that is, developing metrics based on the strategic objectives previously outlined.

Selecting metrics is not a one-time shot and you're finished. It often takes numerous iterations. We choose a metric that we think is correct, only to find out that it also triggers behaviors that we didn't want. So, we adjust and try a different metric, and so on.

One example of metrics and systems failure occurred at a factory that had severe quality problems. Their reject rate was enormous, and the CEO asked us to visit the facility and review their quality systems to find the solutions. They had quality posters and quotes hanging throughout the facility. They had a quality department.

After taking a tour and listening about how quality conscious they were, we asked them the telling question, "How are your employees measured?" Their response was that they were measured on the units produced. So, I asked the follow-up question, "Who fixes the quality issues?" And the answer was that the quality department analyzed the failures at the end of the production process and fixed the problems. In this system, the line workers were not responsible for or rewarded for quality. They were rewarded for pumping out the units. All that mattered to them was the number of units produced, regardless of whether they were good or bad.

The reward system in this facility drove the undesirable behavior of ignoring quality. Failures were never connected to the source of the problem. The employee reward and measurement system was then changed to measure the quality of the units produced, and magically the defect rate shrunk dramatically. Suddenly, employees became more conscious of the quality they produced because it directly affected their paycheck.

10.8.1 Select the Metrics Team

Selecting the metrics team is a step that should not be taken lightly. Selecting the correct individuals can have a major effect on the outcome of the metrics development process. The metrics team should be a small team (5–10 members) consisting of managers from various branches of the organization. The purpose of this team is not only to develop metrics but also to begin building engagement.

Team members should include managers involved in areas such as finance, operations, human resources, marketing, business development, and regional or branch directors. Depending on the size of the organization, it may even be prudent to include team or project managers. The metrics team should also always include at least one member of the executive team. The idea is to select individuals who will be able to provide insight into what types of measurements will guide the organization towards the accomplishment of strategic objectives.

Team members should be individuals who have established themselves as strong influencers in their respective areas of responsibility. In addition to developing metrics, the metrics team members will be required to communicate the value of the metrics and promote their usage throughout the organization. The selection of appropriate team members is the first step in developing organization-wide buy-in.

The metrics team also includes a facilitator. The facilitator should be familiar with the process of developing metrics and should be tactful at guiding the team's progress without controlling the outcome. The team members themselves should be allowed to develop the metrics. The facilitator's responsibility is to educate the team about the process and guide them through it, not to do it for them. If the team members do not feel like they have developed their own metrics, they will not have any sense of ownership of them. The process of creating metrics is just as important as the resulting metrics themselves.

The facilitator should take the time to create an environment that invites open expression of opinions and encourages discussion. Team members should not feel obligated to be part of the team nor feel inconvenienced by their participation in it. Team members should be invited to join the team, not forced. Additionally, at the beginning of the first meeting, the facilitator should take the necessary time to establish a feeling of teamwork and explain the importance of the process in which they are about to engage. Suggestions and opinions should be allowed to be expressed openly to ensure that all perspectives are considered.

10.8.2 Focus on Strategic Objectives

Once the team is selected and an environment of teamwork has been established, it's time to start directing the conversation towards the development of metrics. Start by discussing the strategic vision and how it ties to the strategic mission. Make sure the connection is clear and over-emphasize how the mission supports the realization of the vision. Then, discuss the strategic objectives and explain in very clear terms how the objectives support the mission.

10.8.3 List Potential Metrics

Once the alignment of the vision, mission, and objectives is clear in the team's mind, invite the team to begin discussing potential metrics that will indicate the organization's progress towards strategic objectives. List all the recommended metrics for each strategic objective and avoid eliminating metrics before the lists are complete. At this point, it may be helpful for the facilitator to invite the team to think about some of the changes they would expect to observe as the organization approaches the strategic objectives. Thinking about the observable changes will help the team to identify potential metrics.

10.8.4 Reduce the Lists

Once the team has developed lists of metrics for each strategic objective, the facilitator takes time to discuss metrics and explain the important aspects of good metrics. Take time to discuss the common mistakes made with metrics and how to avoid them. Explain clearly the difference between a KPI and a KBI and why each is needed. Also, discuss and possibly list the characteristics of a good metric. Then, invite the team to begin discussing the lists of potential metrics one objective at a time. Begin to reduce the lists to fewer and fewer metrics. Invite the team to add, edit, eliminate, and combine metrics as they see fit. The goal is to have the lowest number of metrics possible that will drive the performance and encourage the behaviors necessary to accomplish the strategic objectives. However, make sure that each KPI has at least one KBI associated with it. It is the KBIs that directly influence and affect the KPIs; so, if the link isn't there, the effects on the KPIs will be random.

While reducing the lists of metrics, carefully consider any potential undesirable or unintended results that may be produced by the metrics. Perhaps the best way to explain this concept is with an example.

Consider an engineering firm with an objective to increase their profit margin. The firm is concerned because the average utilization rate for staff engineers is at 70%. A KPI is chosen to track the percent utilized or the percent billable for each staff engineer. After 6 months of tracking the percent utilized for each staff engineer, the management team notices that all the staff are now at 100% utilization. However, it is also noticed that the profit margin has not changed. After investigating the situation, it is discovered that the staff engineers have been dragging out projects to fill all of their time. A project that would typically take 28 hours during the week is now taking 40 hours, thus allowing the employee to report 100% utilization for the week.

In this example, the failure to achieve the objective of increasing the profit margin is due to the management team's selection of the wrong KPI. Instead of selecting a KPI and associated goals that would more directly affect the objective, the management team selected a KPI and goals that encouraged bad behavior. Because the staff engineers have no control over how much work they are given to complete each week, the only way they can improve their utilization rate is by making sure the work they are given fills all of their time by working at a slower pace. This, of course, was not the intended result.

Carefully consider each metric and discuss any potential negative impacts of the metric. Will the metric encourage negative behaviors, such as gaming the system? Will the metric cause different teams throughout the organization to compete against each other, instead of working together? Will the metric only be applicable to a small part of the organization, resulting in a feeling of indifference throughout the rest of the organization? Be sure to alter or eliminate metrics that may have negative repercussions.

10.8.5 Fully Define Metrics

Now that the metrics team has selected KPIs and KBIs that are aligned with the strategy and meet the criteria of a good metric, it's important that the team take the time to fully define each metric. Defining the metrics in detail will provide an opportunity for the metrics team to ensure that everyone has the same understanding of the metrics. A fully defined metric is also easier to communicate to the other members of the organization. A metric cannot accomplish what it is meant to accomplish until it has been well defined.

Each metric should have a unique and meaningful name that will make the metric easy to refer to in discussions both at the staff-level and managerial meetings. A captain should be assigned for each metric. This person will act as the authority on this metric and its usage and will also be the lead promoter of the metric for the organization. Each metric should have a detailed description of what it is and how it's calculated. The alignment of the metric to the corporate strategy and its objectives should be clearly described to ensure that everyone understands how the metric supports the common good of the company. Finally, the intended result of the metric and how the resulting data will be used should be clearly described. It is natural for employees to fear and avoid a metric if they think it is just a way for management to decide who to fire. It must be made clear that the metric is a mutually beneficial tool for driving performance and influencing behavior, not for determining layoffs. The following figure is a tabulated summary of a fully defined metric (Chart 10.1).

Name	Provide a unique and meaningful name
Captain	Who will take charge of this metric?
Description	Fully describe the metric in a clear and precise manner
Calculation	Show the calculation associated with metric
Strategic alignment	Explain in detail how this metric will support the corporate strategic plan
Intended result	Describe the intended result of using this metric
Usage	Clearly explain how the data resulting from this metric will be used

CHART 10.1
Fully defined metric.

10.9 SUMMARY

Metrics bring the strategy to life by driving performance and influencing behaviors. When developed effectively, they can become a significant source of motivation, inspiration, and recognition. Remember that organizations will often be required to keep track of all kinds of data. Much of that data is not and should not be treated as a KPI nor a KBI. KPIs and KBIs are those metrics that are essential to executing the strategy. It's important not to confuse everyday business data collection requirements generated by the accounting department or the production scheduling department with KPIs and KBIs.

> We measure lots of things in business. But not all measures are performance measures, and not all measures deserve the same amount of our time and attention. Not all measures need to be acted upon either. Performance measures are a subset of measures that track the results related to our organization's biggest priorities right now.
>
> **Barr, 2014**

11

Action Items and Goals

11.1 INTRODUCTION

The space program and NASA have shifted their focus and there is much confusion in the aerospace industry to determine what they should work on next. The United States is using foreign rockets to launch satellites, and private companies are fighting their way towards becoming the first commercial provider of space transportation, including tourism.

Being tangled up in these struggles finds American aerospace companies in a quandary attempting to redefine themselves. Companies that were once the primary industry in a community are now only supporting a small portion of the population.

One of the authors of this book was brought into a company of this type and was asked to help them redefine themselves. Unfortunately, the company was extremely siloed. The manufacturing silo was in direct conflict with the engineering silo. Engineering felt that the only way to save the company was by coming up with creative technologies, like lift mechanisms into space that didn't require rockets, or hypersonic speed engines. Manufacturing was looking for ways to make cheaper rockets and wasn't interested in wasting time producing engineering's fantasies.

The author organized an off-site strategy workshop where the leadership and senior management were brought together in the hope that a unified plan could be created. It was a disaster because it turned into a power struggle between the various factions of the organization. In the end, they came up with a vision and strategy that cemented the division. The leadership was not forceful enough in their commitment to create a vision that the entire company would need to stand behind. They let the engineering and manufacturing organizations run over them. After this strategy workshop, the author refused to work with them any longer. Since then, the company has seen major declines in their revenues and they are on the verge of bankruptcy. A strong commitment to success starts with leadership and without it, there is no moving forward.

An action item is an isolated task to be completed by one individual or a small team. Action items are typically short-term and are usually completed before some specified follow-up meeting. They support the strategy of the organization by taking distinct steps towards achieving individual or unit goals designed to move the performance needle in the desired direction. Distinct business units will set short-term goals based on strategic objectives and metrics. The goals are then broken down into simple action items, the execution of which will help the unit realize the goals that have been set. Action items can be thought of as the executable steps to accomplishing the unit goals that will improve the strategic business metrics that have been established.

Goals and action items can be developed during strategic planning meetings and then adapted and added to during quarterly executive meetings, monthly management meetings, and weekly or even daily unit or team meetings. Action items and goals should be very clear with a distinct start and finish and should always be written using terminology that applies directly to the individuals responsible for executing the action. There should also be no confusion as to which individuals are responsible for accomplishing the task and who they will report to once the task is completed. The individual reported to should also be the individual holding the purse strings for any changes being made if there are costs involved in completing the action item. This individual gives approval prior to the action taking place and is therefore invested in its success. The individuals responsible for executing the action items and accomplishing the goals should always be involved in their development. Involving all the responsible individuals as a unified group will build ownership of the goals and action items and will increase the likelihood that the goals will be realized.

11.2 CHARACTERISTICS OF EFFECTIVE GOALS

Establishing goals can be a great way to get individuals, teams, and operational units to take incremental steps in the right direction. They can also create a regular sense of accomplishment. The organizational objectives can take a long time to achieve but setting short-term goals that support the longer-term objectives will provide the team with a sense of momentum in the right direction and will provide a regular sense of assurance that their efforts are paying off. Accomplishing short-term goals provides regular opportunities to celebrate the successes of the unit. Goals are also a great way to make the objectives more clearly relatable to the functions and daily tasks of the operational units. In this section, we will use the well-known acronym SMART to discuss the common characteristics of an effective goal. A SMART goal is Specific, Measurable, Achievable, Results-focused, and Time-bound.

11.2.1 Specific

A specific goal is one that does not lend itself to misinterpretation. The goal should be written in clear language specific to those responsible for achieving it. Additionally, the goals should not be conflicting. For example, a goal to speed up production and a goal to improve quality may be conflicting goals unless an action plan is set in place that clearly lays out how to achieve both goals at the same time. Goals should be simple, meaning that they are clearly presented and not overly complicated, but not simplistic, meaning that they are still challenging and result in a true sense of accomplishment when they are achieved.

11.2.2 Measurable

Goals need to be measurable so that those responsible for achieving them will have a clear target and will be able to easily observe their progress towards that target. The results of the efforts of those working towards accomplishing the goal should be visually displayed in real time, and once the goal is achieved, it should be celebrated. Also, one of the most important points about making goals measurable is to remember that "a measurement system does not exist for management information or for costing – it exists for motivation" (Plenert, 1995). If you need to improve production, then measure production. Don't measure what you don't want to motivate. Employees will focus their efforts on whatever it is that you're measuring. This means that not only does every goal need to be measurable, but every measured goal needs to be aligned with strategic objectives. If any goal is not aligned with strategic objectives, then achieving that goal is a waste and not value-adding.

11.2.3 Applicable

Goals need to be applicable to those responsible for achieving them. This may seem obvious, but it is not uncommon for staff members to have goals set for them that they actually have little or no influence over. For example, a staff engineer may have a goal to be 90% billable, but has no control over his or her workload. How can the staff engineer who is just completing assigned tasks possibly control how billable he or she is without direct control over the workload? Who should be responsible to make sure that the engineer has a sufficient amount of work to keep himself or herself at the 90% mark?

In addition to being applicable, goals need to be applied. This means that those responsible for their accomplishment need to have owner-ship of them. Ownership is established by involving those responsible for accomplishing a goal to be involved in establishing the goal in the first place. Then, once the goal is created, it needs to be clearly communicated to the team and progress towards the goal should be visually obvious in real time. Effective goals are always applicable and are applied to those responsible for making them a reality. A goal that is not applicable and is not applied is not a goal but a wish.

11.2.4 Results-Oriented

A results-oriented goal is one that is focused on the outcome of the com-bined efforts, not the individual actions. The goal can be broken down into discrete action items but the goal itself should be focused on the outcome or the result of accomplishing the action items. Results-oriented also means that the unit or the team has an uncompromised focus on achieving results. Focusing on results instills a commitment to making things happen.

11.2.5 Time-Bound

Every goal should have a specified start time and end time. Making a goal time-bound forces the team to design goals that are both achievable yet challenging and creates a sense of accountability.

11.3 ACTION PLAN

Each goal can be broken down into distinct action items. These action items will assign responsibilities to specific individuals who will create

Action plan
Goal statement:

Action item	Responsible party	Start	End	Notes
				Resources needed, expected challenges, desired outcomes, etc.

Action item	Responsible party	Start	End	Notes

CHART 11.1
Action plan.

clear accountability within the group. Each individual should know what part he or she plays in working towards accomplishing the goal. Action items can be organized and displayed in an action plan that will increase the clarity of individual expectations. There are many ways to create an action plan. The above figure is one way to organize an action plan; this template can be customized to the needs of your specific unit (Chart 11.1).

11.4 PRIORITIZING ACTION ITEMS AND GOALS

The lists of action items and goals for each metric can become lengthy and tend to continue to grow over time. As the duration of action items begins to overlap, it will most likely become necessary to begin prioritizing the action items to achieve the best results. Effective prioritization of action items requires an understanding of the impact and the effort associated with each action item. Some action items will have more impact than others. That is, they will tend to move the performance needle further in the right direction. At the same time, some action items will require greater effort than others. Prioritization of action items is a balance of impact and effort. An effective way to prioritize action items is by creating an action item prioritization matrix.

The action item prioritization matrix is developed by assigning each action item a level of impact from 0 to 10 and a level of effort from 0 to 10. Action items are then graphed with the impact on the y-axis and the effort on the x-axis. The graph can be divided into quadrants to more clearly define which tasks have the highest priority. The highest priority

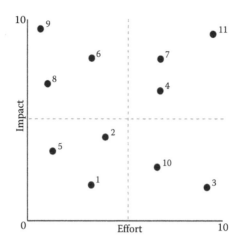

CHART 11.2
Action item prioritization matrix.

would be to complete the tasks that have a high impact and a low required effort. These are the tasks that lie in the upper left quadrant and should be completed first. These are often referred to as "low hanging fruit" which makes them "quick wins" and can be used to demonstrate quick progress. The second set of tasks to be completed would be those in the upper right quadrant. These are the tasks that will have a high impact but require a high amount of effort. The third set of tasks to be completed would be those in the bottom left quadrant which are the tasks that have a lower impact but also require little effort to complete. The tasks that lie in the bottom right quadrant should be given the lowest priority and may not be completed at all. These are the tasks that require a high level of effort and have little impact. The above figure is an example of an action item prioritization matrix (Chart 11.2).

11.5 SUMMARY

Goals and action items are a great way to cascade strategic objectives and metrics down to operational units. They make it clear what actions each individual should be taking to support the vision and mission of the organization. They take seemingly lofty and long-term expectations and break them down into manageable and achievable steps. Remember to stick to the goals and action items you and your team have set. When daily operations become very busy, it is common for the goals and action items to be lost in the day-to-day hustle. However, it is through an enterprise-wide unified strategy that the day-to-day hustle will become more manageable and productive. A team that learns to work together towards achieving common goals will be more likely to reduce the stressful daily firefighting and progress towards a high performing and rewarding culture.

12

Strategy Map

12.1 INTRODUCTION

One of the authors of this book was brought into a factory that produced flexible electronics. It specializes in electroluminescence. This is a plastic product that lights up and can be seen in numerous car and truck dashboard displays. It can also be seen in signage, like in grocery stores and casinos, where electric sockets aren't readily available.

He was brought in as Director of Quality and was given the task of reducing their 13+% defect rate. Because of the high defect rate, the organization overproduced everything. And the losses had an enormous impact on their profitability.

He became very concerned about the lack of direction within the organization. There was no strategy, vision, mission statements which should be used to give the organization focus. There were no valid metrics and it was impossible to say that the changes they made were strategically focused, because of the lack of direction.

He started by insisting on a strategy workshop that needed to be attended by all senior management. In this 2-day workshop, leadership and management were challenged to define the goals and the direction of the organization. They were also challenged to create a New Product Development team, which previously did not exist. And the author insisted on a focus on quality throughout all their messaging.

The next step was to define a set of metrics, which could be used as a scorecard for measuring performance. These metrics would then be funneled down to the associate employees in a form that was relevant and specific to each of their functions, and which gave them direction in their performance.

The strategy workshop was followed up with an action plan, which included a series of workshops on tool training for all associates, primarily focused on the Continuous Improvement dimension of the Shingo Model. All associates were taught how to identify quality failures and how to make improvements. Everyone became responsible for quality.

At this point, we are about 5 months into the organizational transformation because the various workshops took time to schedule in and the author helped establish a "Quality Week" where the entire factory was effectively shut down and the employees were instructed that they could change anything, move anything, and fix anything anywhere in the plant. They had total freedom to make any changes. But the rule that they had to live by was that "they could not produce one bad part." This, of course, threw leadership into a panic, but they trusted the process and allowed "Quality Week" to move forward. Management wasn't that convinced, but they were instructed to fall in line behind leadership.

The cultural transformation had been put into motion, and, despite the resistance of middle management, it moved forward. The first day of "Quality Week" produced zero output. But an unlimited number of changes were made by teams of employees throughout the facility. The second day was a little better in that a few products were produced. By the third day, the plant was above 50% of its normal output. On the fourth and fifth days, they exceeded their previous normal output.

The culture of the organization had been irreversibly transformed. Employees felt trusted and empowered. In the future, if they wanted to fix something, they just went ahead and fixed it. If the change required funding, they went to the manager and reasonable funding for improvements was commonplace.

The end result was that they no longer needed to overproduce in the way they previously were doing. In fact, they experienced about a 20% increase in capacity because they didn't spend as much time producing bad parts or fixing product failures.

In the end, by the eighth month when the author left this assignment, the defect rate was below 2% and because of the cultural shift, it was less than 1% after 12 months.

So, what is the key message here? It is simply that the systems that existed used metrics and encouraged behaviors that didn't support the company's goals. There was no strategy system giving employees focus. There was no measurement system which gave employees direction. There was no training system teaching employees the basics of quality and continuous improvement. And there was no New Product Development system giving the company a future and longevity. The strategy systems for this organization had to be rebuilt using the concepts found in this book and through these changes, the culture of the organization was able to be transformed.

Now that the corporate strategy has been developed, it's time to organize the strategy into a strategy map. A strategy map is an effective way to organize the strategy into a concise summary that makes the links between the different aspects of the strategy clearer. The development of a strategy is not completed until it's organized in a way that allows it to be easily communicated and effectively executed.

12.2 BENEFITS OF THE STRATEGY MAP

The primary benefit of creating a strategy map is that it is a great way to organize all the major aspects of the strategy into a concise format. Organizing the strategic plan makes it more manageable and executable. A strategy that can be organized into a simple and concise format will accomplish much more than a strategy that fills an entire 3-inch binder.

Once the strategy is organized into a concise strategy map, it can quickly and simply be communicated throughout the organization. The organization of the strategy map makes it easy to quickly locate the information needed and helps all members of the organization see how they fit into the strategy. It also prevents operational units from losing sight of the big picture of what the organization is working to accomplish. Keeping the big picture in mind helps direct decision-makers as they work to guide their teams. Not only does an organized strategy map improve communication but it also prevents miscommunication and misdirection.

12.3 DETAILS OF THE STRATEGY MAP

The strategy map begins with an explanation of the strategic direction of the organization, which consists of guiding principles, core competencies, vision, mission, and a definition of the customer. Presenting this information as part of the strategy map develops a common understanding of why the organization exists and where it's heading. Establishing a common direction for the organization is critical for ensuring a united effort to support the purpose of the organization.

Strategic direction			
Guiding principles:			
Core competencies:			
Vision:			
Mission:			
Defining the customer:			
The strategy map			
Perspective:			
Priorities	Objectives	Metrics	Goals and action items
Priority statement: End state statement: Goal statement:	Objective statement:	Metrics statement(s):	Goal statement(s): Action item(s):
	Objective statement:	Metrics statement(s):	Goal statement(s): Action item(s):
	Objective statement:	Metrics statement(s):	Goal statement(s): Action item(s):

CHART 12.1
Strategy map.

Next, the strategy is broken down into priorities, objectives, metrics, goals, and action items. By organizing strategic information in this format, the connections between the different aspects of the strategy become clear. There should be a clear line of sight from action items all the way up to the vision. This provides each member of the organization with a clear understanding of how his or her actions are supporting the vision of the organization. Although there are many different ways to format a strategy map, the above is a general format that can be added to and adapted as needed for your organization. The example shows a strategy map for just one strategic perspective. However, your map should be extended to include all the strategic perspectives discussed in Chapter 8. Also, for your strategy map, it may be necessary to adjust the number of priorities, objectives, metrics, goals, and action items. The strategy map presented in the above figure is an adaptation of the map presented in the book, *World Class Manager* (Plenert, 1995) (Chart 12.1).

12.4 USING THE STRATEGY MAP TO BUILD BUY-IN

Building buy-in is not a step in the process, but rather it's a critical element of the strategic planning process that is woven into every step along the way. Building buy-in is the process of creating a desire in all members of the organization to support the strategic plan. The goal is to develop a widespread sense of ownership of the strategy so that all members of the organization feel excited about the strategy, rather than feel like it is simply being forced upon them. A strategy that is quickly thrown together by a few executives behind closed doors and then thrust upon the organization will be greeted with contempt and will generate little to no real momentum as it is executed. The strategic planning and management process must take advantage of every opportunity to build buy-in from the very beginning.

A great way to keep the momentum going to build buy-in is to post a draft of the strategy map in a common area and invite all members of the organization to stop by and view it. A few members of the strategic planning team may want to be available to explain the strategy map and answer questions. The map should remain posted long enough for the majority of the members of the organization to stop by. Members of the organization should be invited to view the strategy at their convenience but should not be obligated. Those who do stop by should be invited to provide feedback. Feedback can be provided by talking to any member of the strategic planning team, by dropping suggestions in a suggestions box, or by writing notes directly on the strategy map if the map is printed large enough. All feedback should be carefully considered for incorporation into the strategy. This type of event is referred to as a "Measures Gallery" by Stacey Barr in her book, *Practical Performance Measurement* (Barr, 2014), where she discusses the details of conducting this type of event and the beneficial effect it can have on developing enterprise-wide buy-in.

A strategy lacking buy-in will never have a chance to develop momentum. It will end up on a shelf collecting dust until the following year when a new strategy is developed. No one will care about the strategy until individuals know they have ownership in it.

12.5 SUMMARY

It can be tempting to simplify the process of defining the strategy by reusing an ineffective strategy from the past or by filling out some online strategy template. Avoid the temptation to shorten the process at all costs. The process of defining the strategy, if done correctly, can be just as important as the strategy itself. The defining process creates buy-in and ownership and will begin to ignite excitement for the new strategy. Simply using a generic strategy is ineffective because it encourages a similar attitude of complacency and indifference to spread throughout the organization.

Your organization's strategy should be a customized, carefully crafted, focal point that will generate passion throughout all levels of the organization. Too often, a strategy is treated like a spare tire that is only used when the organization seems to be in trouble. However, an effective strategy is more like a steering wheel that is used to direct the organization down a successful path. Remember: You will receive the same amount of care and attention out of a strategic plan that you put into it.

Now that so much time and attention have been dedicated to developing an outstanding strategic plan, what do you do with it? File it away? E-mail it to everyone so that it will sit in their inbox for weeks until they forget it's there? Phase III will focus on how to successfully execute a strategic plan and align the entire organization with that plan. Fortunately, because the strategy has been developed in a way that buy-in has already been established and all aspects of the strategy are linked, the process of executing the strategy and aligning the organization with the strategy will flow more naturally.

Phase III

Execute: Engaging and Aligning the Organization

13

Introduction to Execute

Unless you are heading straight for your objectives, the most heroic efforts in the world will only be as effective as the component of work directly related to your goals. Indeed, when carrying out improvements, you will only be truly effective when you first set your objectives and then head straight for them.

Shigeo Shingo
The Sayings of Shigeo Shingo, p. 53

13.1 INTRODUCTION

NUMMI was a joint venture between General Motors in the United States and Toyota from Japan. There were many struggles in blending the two management styles, and there have been numerous books published about the United States perspective of this merger. One interesting story that came out of this implementation occurred when a Japanese executive came to visit the NUMMI plant in the San Francisco Bay Area. He was walking through the facility on a plant tour with an American executive and he asked the American, "What problems are you having in the plant?"

The General Motors' executive's response was, "We're not having any problems. Things have been running very smoothly."

The Toyota executive turned to the American, shook his finger at him, and said, "No Problem is Problem!"

The job of the leader is to search for opportunities for improvement. It's the leader's job to focus continuously on making things better. His job is to search for systems and behavior shortcomings. If the leader/executive

134 • Strategic Excellence in the AEC Industry

isn't working on a problem, then he or she is simply not doing his or her job. Hence, "No Problem is Problem."

If you want to read a detailed account of the NUMMI implementation from the Japanese/Toyota perspective, take a look at the book, *Toyota's Global Marketing Strategy: Innovation through Breakthrough Thinking and Kaizen*, Taylor and Francis Group, CRC Press, 2017, and authored by Kouichiro Noguchi, a former director of Toyota; Shozo Hibino, the co-author of the "Breakthrough Thinking" series; and Gerhard Plenert, an author of this current book.

Now that the strategic plan has been developed based on the outcomes of a thorough analysis, it's time to move from planning the strategy to the task of managing the strategy. Strategic management involves both execution of the strategy and refinement of the strategy over time. The Execute phase is crucial for making the strategy a reality.

You may have noticed that considerable effort has been dedicated to creating a strategic plan. The resulting plan is highly customized and unique to the organization and the environment in which it is operating. Had the plan not been carefully prepared, the execution of it would be an impossible feat. A strategy that has been customized specifically for the organization responsible for executing it will be better received and will be more likely to drive the organization to an exciting future. In other words, effective execution of a strategic plan requires that the plan is designed specifically for the organization. A generic strategic plan will face passionate and well-grounded opposition from the organization because the members of the organization will quickly recognize that it is not right for them. The Analyze and Define phases have worked to develop a strategic plan that is well prepared for the Execute phase. Execution without proper planning will result in confusion, and planning without effective execution will result in unrealized wishful thinking.

> Execution is the ability to mesh strategy with reality, align people with goals, and achieve promised results.
>
> **Lawrence Bossidy**

13.2 WHY EXECUTE?

It may seem obvious that your strategy needs to be executed. Surprisingly, the Execute phase is one that is often completely overlooked. Leaders of organizations often work diligently to develop a detailed and elegant strategic plan and then assume that the rest of the organization will recognize its value and execute based on it. Those who have worked so hard to create the strategic plan often feel that they've done their part and now it's up to everyone else to make it happen.

It is also common for many of the lower-level members of organizations to assume that the strategy is not for them. They see it as something that the executive managers are dealing with but that they don't actually need to pay attention to. They put their heads down and focus on the tasks associated with their jobs and rarely take the time to look around to see if their actions are making a difference. If staff members are not actively engaged in the execution process they will most likely never get involved.

The Execute phase is also often overlooked because it is not a simple step that can quickly be accomplished in the strategic process. The Execute phase is an ongoing process, not a onetime event. It requires continued effort by every member of the organization which can require a great deal of communication and coordination. It can require managers to exercise some emotional intelligence as they encourage their staff to engage with the strategy and incentivize them to take ownership of strategic outcomes. Executing the strategy requires constant renewal and encouragement to keep the organization aligned with strategic objectives, as described in the following:

> A strategy, even a great one, doesn't implement itself.
>
> **Jeroen De Flander**

13.3 APPROACH TO EXECUTE

The process of executing the strategy requires constant attention to ensure that the organization remains engaged with the strategy. It requires that new members of the organization are converted to the strategy and that the strategy is clearly communicated throughout the organization. The Execute phase is facilitated by the concepts listed in the following figure (see Chart 13.1).

CHART 13.1
Strategic Excellence Model – Execute Phase.

13.4 SUMMARY

Weak execution of even a fantastic strategy can result in failure. The Execute phase is the critical ongoing process of making strategy a reality. Execution does not happen on its own. It requires constant and consistent attention to enterprise alignment and cultural engagement. Exceptional leaders do not simply dictate a plan and then sit back and hope it is realized. Their visionary leadership is accompanied by an empowering approach to effective execution.

> A vision and strategy aren't enough. The long-term key to success is Execution. Each day. Every day.
>
> **Richard M. Kovacevich**

14

Cascading

14.1 INTRODUCTION

Kiichiro Toyoda, a founder of Toyota Motor company, thought that the making of products to satisfy customers requires a systemic approach of doing work that will cover the entire processes, ranging from identifying customers' needs to including engineering development, design, production, inspection, logistics, services, and maintenance. He also believed that the goal of customer satisfaction could not be obtained unless Toyota could improve all processes in a continuous manner. This thinking habit has become the foundation of the current Toyota technique referred to as "Kaizen" (every time improvement, everywhere improvement, every one improvement; continuous improvement).

Cascading the corporate strategy is all about making it relevant to every individual in the organization. Many high-level objectives and metrics may not seem directly applicable to every unit within the organization. There may be some units, especially administrative units, that don't feel they have a way of supporting the strategy. They may see their function as something that just must get done and can't be improved to support strategic objectives. The focus of cascading the strategy is to bring the strategy down through the organization, level by level, and make it relevant to every member of the organization. To develop long-term Strategic Excellence, every member of the organization must have a clear understanding of how his or her performance and behaviors affect the organization as a whole.

14.2 CASCADING VS. FRAGMENTING

It's common for some units within the organization to feel left out of the strategy if they don't understand how they can affect it. When this happens, they will most likely develop their own objectives and metrics that are designed to help them improve their operations but do not necessarily have any impact on the successful execution of the corporate strategy. This action is usually referred to as fragmentation. Organizational units typically don't see this type of fragmentation as an issue because the improvements they are making are beneficial within their own scope of practice. The danger of fragmentation is that you end up with many isolated achievements throughout the organization, but they don't add up to much progress overall. As an illustration, think of a natural watershed. There may be many natural springs scattered throughout the watershed. Each spring produces a good result. However, in order for the individual values of each spring to make a significant impact on the landscape of the watershed, all the springs must run together into creeks and then into a river. A full flowing river carries with it significant energy, but the river depends on all the contributions of the smaller creeks and springs. If all the creeks and springs were fragmented and running in all different directions, the river would never be able to reach its full potential.

Cascading means that the strategy map is conveyed to each unit at every level of the organization and is made applicable to the specific function of that unit. Every individual should have a clear understanding of how his or her actions and behaviors will impact the strategic objectives and metrics. This is often referred to as a clear "line of sight" from individual actions to strategic objectives. Cascading creates strategic coordination between functional units, meaning that each unit has an understanding of how their performance and behaviors will impact the operations of other units and the success of the organization as a whole. Individual units will often need to develop their own strategic action items and goals, but those unit-specific action items and goals must have a clear and direct path to the strategic objectives and metrics.

Fragmentation results from a lack of enterprise-wide focus, which creates confusion and frustration throughout the organization. A lack of focus can result in constantly changing targets as individuals and operational units attempt to achieve goals that they think will be beneficial to the organization but don't ever seem to result in the recognition they expect to receive. Employees begin to feel indifferent to goals and action items because achieving them doesn't seem to accomplish much and the direction coming from management seems to change on a regular basis anyway.

Cascading creates a strategic focus at every level. It provides each operational unit and individual employee with a clear direction that will guide decision making, unit-level goal setting, and the development of action items. Cascading creates the focus necessary to prioritize tasks and separate the necessary from the unnecessary. Strategic focus not only guides what to do but also what not to do. Achieving the best outcomes often requires reassigning resources currently dedicated to activities that only offer mediocre outcomes.

> Focus saves huge amounts of process time, builds worker morale, and creates the right conditions to reap timely results. So why, given the benefits, is focus so difficult to achieve? I've found that the problem lies in the fact that many organizations prioritize based on politics, turf, or squeaky wheel behavior; manage their priorities too loosely so that it's easy for new distractions to push them aside; or, in more cases than many will admit, don't prioritize to begin with. The result is that few organizations actively choose to do a few activities and therefore not do dozens of others.
>
> **Martin, 2012**

14.3 SYNERGY OF CASCADING

Synergy is when people working together are able to accomplish more than they could have accomplished working separately. It's when $x + x > 2x$. Developing synergy within an organization requires a shared vision and a universal commitment to common values. In other words, it requires that everyone in the organization desires the same future and will abide by the same guiding principles to achieve it. A shared vision and universal guiding principles means that the decisions and behaviors of every member of the organization will help to move the group in the same direction within the same constraints. However, if any unit within the group loses sight of the shared vision or begins to act outside the bounds set by the guiding principles, the organization ceases to act as a synergistic whole and will begin to experience fragmentation. The best way to establish or restore synergy within an organization is to reinforce the shared vision and guiding principles by cascading the strategy through all levels of the organization.

> Synergy – the bonus that is achieved when things work together harmoniously.
>
> **Mark Twain**

━━━━━━━━━━

14.4 CASCADING PROCESS

There are many approaches to cascading the strategy to all levels of the organization, and most of the approaches seem to be effective. Some organizations use a top-down approach, others use a bottom-up approach, and others seem to start the cascading process from the center of the organization and move out. Cascading responsibilities can also be divided up by organizational hierarchy, operational units, or geographical region. The most important notion about cascading is to execute a well-organized plan for cascading the strategy, instead of expecting it to cascade itself.

In general, the process for cascading the strategy throughout the organization is as follows:

- Develop a well-organized cascading plan
- Select strategy champions at each level and each unit
- Involve the staff in cascading efforts

In developing a cascading plan, think about what will work best for your specific organization. The goal is to reach every individual within the organization. In some cases, it may be most effective to cascade the strategy by geographical region and select a champion for each branch office. In other cases, cascading by operational function may be more effective because staff may have a better relationship with operational unit leaders, rather than geographical leaders. Whatever approach your organization feels will be most effective, define a cascading plan for the organization and use the selected approach to choose strategy champions.

The strategy champion will be responsible for creating a clear line of sight from each individual to the high-end strategic direction as defined by the strategy map. This will include the creation of goals and action items that have clear connections to strategic objectives. Every staff member should be involved in the process of applying the corporate strategy to his or her individual responsibilities. Goals and action items should never be assigned but should be developed with the help of those responsible for carrying out the action items.

A great way to visualize the cascading process comes from *The 8 – Strategy Execution Model* developed by Jcroen De Flander (https://jeroen-de-flander.com). Chart 14.1 shows the process of cascading the strategy down from the organizational level, to the division level, and

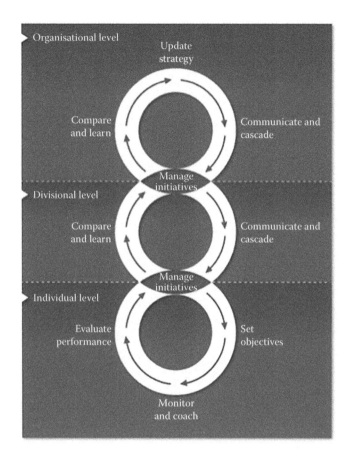

CHART 14.1
The 8 – Strategy Execution Model by Jeroen De Flander.

to the individual level. Then, feedback is sent back up the line. Although the following figure by Jeroen De Flander shows the strategy cascaded by organizational hierarchy, similar imagery could be used to visualize strategy cascading by operational function or geographical location.

14.5 SUMMARY

A strategy, not fully cascaded throughout the organization, will never be able to reach its full potential. A strategy fully cascaded can create an organization-wide synergy and strategic focus, which means that members of the organization working together can accomplish far more than they ever could working independently. Cascading the plan throughout the organization is critical to the effective execution of the plan. Make sure you have a clear plan of how your organization will cascade the strategy. Developing a clear cascading plan will help clarify how unit managers are expected to align their unit with the strategy. This will help prevent fragmentation and promote a culture of synergy throughout the organization.

Time management is dead; in our day the true struggle is focus management.

Dave Crenshaw

15

Governance

15.1 INTRODUCTION

Governance is the process set in place to guide decision making at all levels throughout the organization. Although this book has discussed many different tools and practices that are used to implement effective strategic governance, this chapter focuses more on how to execute "good governance," that is, how to guide decision making without causing harm.

15.2 RISKS OF BAD GOVERNANCE

Bad governance is any type of governance that causes harm, either intentional or unintentional, within the organization or outside the organization. The effects of bad governance can vary significantly and can range from minor dissatisfaction to a complete failure of the organization and, in extreme cases, can even lead to legal consequence. In general, many of the consequences of bad governance fall into two categories. The first is financial and the second is cultural.

Bad governance can have project impacts, such as failure to maintain schedules or failure to complete projects within budget. It can also have impacts on client relationships as clients begin to lose confidence in the effective governance of the organization. Bad governance within the organization will inevitably affect external relationships. Bad governance can also be a source of weak or unstable financial performance. Then, the desire to improve financial performance under a system of bad governance will often lead to dishonesty and the corruption of financial figures.

Unfortunately, the leaders of some organizations think that bad governance will go unnoticed and they expect employees to produce success without proper governance. This approach will place an excessive burden on the members of the organization to compensate for a failure on the part to the governing body. Bad governance is not something that can be hid, and the resulting cultural effects can be significant. As the members of the organization witness bad governance practices, they will begin to split into silos and some members of the organization will abandon ship to join competing firms or start their own competing firms.

It is not uncommon from time to time to read news stories of large and seemingly successful organizations that suddenly fail because of bad governing practices. Stakeholders are becoming more concerned about governance and many potential clients are becoming less likely to do business with organizations that have a history of bad governance practices. Any organization that expects to execute a successful long-term strategy cannot afford to participate in bad governance practices at any level.

15.3 CHARACTERISTICS OF GOOD GOVERNANCE

Good governance creates a solid organization that employees are proud to work for and clients feel confident working with. Good governance practices develop stability and growth within the organization and a reputation of excellence outside the organization. There are many great lists of good governance practices and much research is being dedicated to this area of study. However, most good governance practices seem to fall within one of two categories. The two primary categories of good governance practices are those that are empowering and those that create transparency.

Empowering governance practices are those that guide decision making rather than dictate it. They're practices that encourage what the Shingo Institute refers to as "ideal behaviors" and establish what Stephen Covey called a "moral compass." The idea is that empowered employees have the liberty to make decisions pertaining to their scope of work, and those decisions are guided by empowering governance, rather than being micromanaged by oppressive governance. Empowering governance creates collective participation and an inclusive win-win culture that will create opportunities for growth and innovation that coercive governance practices will never be able to achieve, as expressed in the following:

Treat employees like they make a difference and they will.

Jim Goodnight

Leaders become great, not because of their power, but because of their ability to empower others.

John Maxwell

Transparent governance practices are those that remove secrecy and create integrity. These practices create a sense of equitable treatment allowing all employees the opportunity to enhance their careers. Transparent governance practices also create accountability so that all members of the organization understand what is expected of them and have regular opportunities to report their successes and challenges. Transparent governance practices develop a culture of absolute integrity.

A company that implements good governance practices will quickly stand out as the type of organization that always treats people right. It becomes an organization that clients want to do business with because they know they can have confidence in the service they're paying for.

The following chapter will discuss two of the primary tools in an organization-wide governance process: the scorecard and the dashboard.

15.4 PERFORMANCE REVIEWS

An important tool commonly used in governance plans is the performance review. There exist many ideas about what a performance review should consist of and how it should be carried out. Each organization should develop a method that is customized to the conditions of the organization and the needs of the employees. What works well for one organization may not necessarily work well for another. In this section, we will discuss a few of the most important aspects of a great performance review program. These concepts should be applied as you work to develop a program customized for your organization. These concepts fall into two main categories which are timing and content.

The timing of performance reviews can vary widely. Originally, it seemed that performance reviews were conducted at the end of each year and were tied to an end-of-year bonus. This approach encourages employees to be less worried about their performance during the first half of the year, and then, they tend to ramp up their performance as the performance review gets closer. This, of course, is not the desired result of conducting performance reviews. In other cases, performance reviews seem to never be conducted at all. Instead, the manager simply tells employees that his door is always open. This approach typically results in performance issues not being discussed until they become unbearable. This situation creates a culture of fear because employees appear to be let go even though there was never an issue with their performance. An ideal approach to timing performance reviews is to have quarterly formal performance review meetings with ongoing informal check-ins and real-time feedback. The formal meeting is used to focus on documenting expectations and provide formal recognition of successes while the ongoing check-ins are where most of the progress happens. This approach makes performance reviews seem less like something the manager is just required to do and, instead, shows genuine interest in the success of each employee.

The content of performance reviews should be focused on goal setting and personal development. It shouldn't just focus on recent events but should feel more like a continuation of the last performance review. A positive relationship of genuine interest and trust should be developed, and the employee should be given an opportunity to prepare for the meeting by being given advanced notice of what will be discussed. The discussion should be a reemphasis of information and not necessarily new information. In other words, when an issue arises, it should be discussed with the employee immediately and reemphasized at the next performance review, rather than waiting for the next performance review to bring it up. Feedback should be honest, and goals and expectations should be clear and specific to facilitate self-evaluation. The employee's personal development plan should be discussed and should be considered a major part of the performance review. The employee needs to know that his or her career ambitions are important to the organization and that the organization is supporting those ambitions. If appropriate, a performance improvement plan can be developed for struggling employees to help motivate and document improvements. Remember to give the employee plenty of time to talk. One of the most effective ways to influence others is by listening with the aim of understanding. Finally, recognition of successes should be genuine, and real appreciation should be expressed.

Performance reviews can be a powerful tool in your governance toolbox. They can help to develop a high-performing culture, and they help establish individual ownership of strategic objectives and metrics. They also demonstrate a genuine desire for employees to succeed and achieve their career ambitions. Communicating honest feedback is critical to strategic success.

15.5 SUMMARY

Good governance starts with good leaders who can take on the responsibility of doing what is best for the organization and those affected by it. Through good governance, an empowering culture can be developed that will promote good decision making throughout the organization. Good governance creates an entire organization of good decision-makers, rather than just one or a few, as reflected in this excerpt:

> People's participation is the essence of good governance.
>
> **Narendra Modi**

16

Reporting

16.1 INTRODUCTION

Effective execution of the organization's strategy requires a well-organized and consistently implemented reporting methodology to maintain an organization-wide focus on the strategy. Regular reporting of metrics will help keep the organization moving towards achieving strategic objectives and will help enhance the sense of ownership that was initiated during the Define Phase. Regular reporting also creates accountability and provides an opportunity for managers to express appreciation when performance levels are high and encourage a renewal of effort when performance levels are low.

An important aspect of reporting is to remember that the reporting process is never used to punish, reprimand, or place blame. Reporting is part of the metrics process, which is used to drive performance and stimulate ideal behaviors. The metrics used in the reporting process should be the same metrics agreed on during the creation of the strategy map. Incorporating new metrics creates confusion in the goal. Making the reporting process a negative experience will inevitably destroy its effectiveness and will likely do more harm than good.

This chapter will focus on two primary reporting methods, the balanced scorecard and the operational dashboard. Both methods have been well developed and have proven effective for numerous organizations around the globe. Using these methods will provide a consistent reporting process so that every reporting manager will come to meetings speaking the same language. Using a consistent reporting method generates effective communication. Using the Lean A3 reporting tool to support the details behind each dashboard activity and metric may also be useful (the A3 will be discussed in a later chapter in this book). These reporting methodologies will help maintain a focus on strategic metrics and objectives.

16.2 BALANCED SCORECARD

The balanced scorecard is a strategic management tool for reporting the performance of the organization or division based on a select few business metrics. The "balanced" in balanced scorecard suggests that the report should balance financial with nonfinancial metrics, thus reducing the narrow-mindedness of purely financial reporting methodologies. The balanced scorecard focuses on how well the organization is executing the strategy. All the metrics included on the balanced scorecard should come directly from the strategic plan and should be grouped by objective, priority, and perspective to make it clear how well the organization is supporting the strategy and which areas may need work. The metrics on the balanced scorecard should be selected from all four strategic perspectives, which are financial, operational, employee, and customer.

One of the strengths of the balanced scorecard method is that it aligns the corporate strategy with actual reporting in an organized manner. In other words, it aligns strategic planning with strategic management and makes sure they are focused on achieving the same outcomes. It provides actionable follow-up and accountability for the strategic plan. The balanced scorecard is a broad top-down approach that links short-term performance to long-term vision, thus helping to remove the siloed blinders from individual functional units within the organization.

A well-designed balanced scorecard should communicate concisely all the necessary information. Information should be presented using a dashboard with visual displays that allow the reader to understand the information within a few minutes. In general, a balanced scorecard should be kept to one page and should only contain the most critical strategic metrics. The balanced scorecard is meant to be used at annual, semiannual, and quarterly executive meetings or possibly even monthly division meetings but is not as effective when used for daily or weekly reporting. It is not designed to provide large amounts of data, but rather to provide a quick look into strategic performance levels. Any areas of concern can be analyzed further as needed, but the balanced scorecard is designed to identify those areas and help to aim corrective actions.

The balanced scorecard can be thought of as a medical chart located at the foot of a patient's bed. The medical chart will contain information from many sources, such as various nurses, laboratories, medical imaging facilities, and pharmacies. A doctor will review the chart on entering the patient's room to get a quick understanding of how the patient is doing. The doctor won't read through the entire patient's history but will quickly look at the most vital information pertaining to the condition and expectations relating to that patient. If any information seems unfavorable, the doctor will investigate further and may contact one of the sources to learn more about what has transpired since the last time the doctor observed the patient. The balanced scorecard is meant to do the same. It provides managers with a quick look at the "vital signs" of the organization and points out any areas that may need further investigation. Many great examples of balanced scorecards and software exist online but remember that the most important aspect of your own scorecard is that it must be based on your own organization's strategy and should only include the metrics that would be considered "vital signs" based on the metrics selected in your strategy and based on the conditions and expectations relating to your organization. Don't allow any software or template to dictate what belongs on your dashboard.

16.3 OPERATIONAL DASHBOARD

The operational dashboard report can be thought of as "deep dive" into the organization's metrics specific to the area being analyzed. It is meant to contain more detailed information on how that branch of the organization is performing. Each operational unit will typically have its own operational dashboard. When the balanced scorecard report indicates a problem, the operational dashboard will provide managers with more detailed information to further analyze the problem.

Operational dashboards will focus more on daily and weekly performance and less on monthly or quarterly performance. The operational dashboard will contain more objectives, goals, and action items than the few, high-level items contained in the balanced scorecard. The goals and action items of the operational dashboard will be reviewed weekly, daily, or even hourly, focusing on the performance measures that were selected earlier in your strategy. Whereas the balanced scorecard is thought of as containing the "vital signs" of the organization, the operational dashboard can be thought of as the hourly detailed nurse's notes, lengthy test results, lists of medications and when they're due, etc.

Operational dashboards should be posted in highly visible places so that staff members can see them regularly. They should act as real-time indicators of how the operational unit is doing. In this way, they become focused motivators driving the organization towards the desired results. The operational dashboard should answer questions such as: "How are we performing right now?" "How are we performing today?" "Are we on track to meet our goals today?" "Are we on track to meet our goals this week?" "What action items do we have left to complete and how much longer do we have to complete them?" Operational dashboards should be easy to read and easy to use. They can be as simple as checking a box in a table on a whiteboard every time a task is complete.

The next level of detail below the dashboard is the Lean A3 report, which details all the activities that are associated with each strategic initiative. The A3 will be discussed in more detail in a later chapter of this book.

Remember that, like the balanced scorecard, the operational dashboard must be linked to the strategy of the organization. Although the operational dashboard may contain many additional daily and weekly goals and action items, they must all be aligned with the strategic objectives and metrics outlined in the strategy map. Also, remember that this report cannot be used to punish or tear down individuals within the unit, but is meant to bring the unit together to accomplish more than they could have working apart. It is meant to drive performance and inspire ideal behaviors within the unit.

16.4 SUMMARY

Reporting is not just for the sake of having something to discuss in our meetings. It's not just so we can sit around and talk about what the data say. Remember that you don't just analyze the performance data, you also create the performance data. What this means is that reporting is for the sake of acting, not the other way around. If the reporting isn't motivating performance and stimulating ideal behaviors, then what good is it? Additionally, if our reporting isn't working to move all operational units towards achieving the same vision, then our reporting is not doing its job.

This chapter has discussed two great tools for helping facilitate the governance and reporting process in your organization. Although these tools have been proven to be highly effective, they must be used correctly. Remember that the purpose of using these reporting tools is to drive performance, influence behaviors, and align the entire organization with the corporate strategy.

17

Engagement

It has long been understood that our beliefs have a profound effect on our behavior. What is often overlooked, however, is the equally profound effect that systems have on behavior.

Shigeo Shingo

17.1 INTRODUCTION

A highly engaged workforce is one that not only has a sense of ownership of the corporate strategy but is also excited to support it. Building engagement focuses on creating an organization whose members take pride in their work and experience a sense of satisfaction in being great at what they do. An engaged workforce will not only have increased job satisfaction but will also have a higher level of job performance, a better attitude towards solving problems, a healthier culture, and a more synergist team atmosphere.

There is a great deal that organizations can do to foster employee engagement. There is also a great deal that organizations often do that hinder or destroy employee engagement. Too often, when organizations suffer from a lack of employee engagement, the executive team assumes it is due to a poorly motivated workforce. It is critical to understand that a low level of employee engagement is only a symptom, it is not the actual problem itself. If employees who are already suffering from low levels of engagement are treated like they are the problem, the levels of employee engagement will inevitably plummet even further. A lack of employee engagement is always an indicator of a problem with the system, not with the employees. Thus, building employee engagement requires a systems approach. That is, it requires changes to the system in which the employees are working, not trying to force change directly on the employees.

In this chapter, we'll explore three keys to a highly engaged workforce. These keys are meant to act as a guide, not as a prescription. Every organization is unique and requires customized solutions. As you look for ways to improve your system in order to foster high levels of employee engagement, keep these concepts in mind. Focus on a holistic systems approach by thinking about how your decisions and actions will affect the organization as a whole. The three keys to a highly engaged workforce are organizational purpose, individual value, and progress.

17.2 ORGANIZATIONAL PURPOSE

An engaged workforce is built on the foundation of an engaging purpose. In previous chapters, we've discussed how to develop an inspiring vision and a meaningful mission as part of the strategic planning process. However, developing the vision and mission is only the beginning. The organizational purpose needs to become more than just a wall hanging. It must become real. It must become believable.

The purpose of the organization needs to benefit not only the bottom line but also the members of the organization and the community. It should be something that employees will feel good about dedicating their time, energy, and attention to. Also, the organizational purpose must remain always present and should be evident at the core of everything the organization does. An organization that is not highly engaged in its own purpose cannot expect its employees to be highly engaged in the organization, as expressed in the following manner:

> I think if the people who work for a business are proud of the business they work for, they'll work that much harder, and therefore, I think turning your business into a real force for good is good business sense as well.
>
> **Richard Branson**

17.3 INDIVIDUAL VALUE

Individual value means that each employee recognizes the value of his or her role in the organization and this individual value is validated by the way the employee is treated within the organization. Establishing individual value can be the difference between an organization of employees who do the minimum to keep their jobs and an organization of employees who take great pride in their efforts to contribute to the forward motion of the organization.

During the industrial age, many organizations developed a tendency to treat employees as easily replaceable and viewed them as an expense. However, in the current information age, employees are more than ever the most valuable asset the organization has. AEC firms that attract and retain the top talent will be more likely to outperform other firms. Indicative of this problem is that in the accounting systems utilized in the United States, employees are a "cost" and inventory is an asset, causing the mind-set that costs should be minimized and assets should be increased. In Japan, we find just the reverse. Standing inventory is a cost and employees are an asset. Just consider how this one difference changes the approach and treatment of employees.

Highly educated and skilled employees know their value and will naturally be attracted to the organizations that appreciate that value. Employees who are treated as though they are easy to replace will treat the job as though it is also easy to replace. Employees who are highly valued will respond by, in turn, holding their position with the organization in very high regard.

> Everybody is a genius. But if you judge a fish by its ability to climb a tree, it will live its whole life believing that it is stupid.
>
> **Albert Einstein**

> When I know the leaders in my organization, believe in them, encourage them, and help them to succeed, it helps to strengthen their belief in themselves. I try to help them win increasingly larger victories. People almost always rise to meet your level of expectations. Believe in them, and they will rise to fulfill that belief.
>
> **Maxwell, 2005**

17.4 PROGRESS

An inspiring purpose and a culture of valuing employees need to be accompanied by genuine progress. This progress needs to exist at both the organizational level as well as the individual level. It should be clearly evident that the organization is making advances towards accomplishing its mission. Organizational progress should be visual, and successes should be celebrated. Being a part of a successful organization with an exciting future creates a sense of pride among employees who have been involved in the organization's success. Knowing that the organization is progressing also provides the employees with a sense of security and an exciting future. When employees feel good about the progress and future of the organization, they will be excited to contribute to and be a part of that future.

In addition to the progress of the organization, the individual employees need to experience genuine progress in their careers as a result of being engaged with the organization. This means that employees should be gaining knowledge and developing new skills. They should be progressing through the organization. It is critical that the organization supports employees in their personal goals and efforts to become great at what they do. Employees should have personal development plans, and the organization should be involved in helping employees succeed in realizing their career goals. When an organization supports the progress of its employees, the employees will respond by supporting the progress of the organization as well.

> If everyone is moving forward together, then success takes care of itself.
>
> **Henry Ford**

17.5 A CULTURAL TRANSFORMATION STORY

The O.C. Tanner Company of Salt Lake City, Utah is a Shingo Prize Winner and one of the stories they share has been incorporated into the courses that the Shingo Institute teaches through its affiliates. Gary Peterson, Executive VP, Supply Chain & Production tells how when they began their lean journey 25 years ago, their culture was autocratic and controlling. People just did what they were told using their hands and not their brains.

For management, it became important to change the mind-set of our people. They started a transformation that changed some systems to help people realize they could have an impact on the important metrics. They started with a team-based merit system. Initially, they changed the system so that people would understand that as they improved quality and efficiency and contributed to their team, they would get a raise. It took about 8 months before every team and every individual was driving hard on the things that matter to us, that is, on the metrics.

They used this weekly merit system for about 3 years and it was working well. But they had a problem with cross training. Everyone did one job and it was the only thing they wanted to do. They decided to motivate employees to learn multiple job skills. They changed the compensation system by telling employees that as they learn these different job skills, they'll get a raise. Employees immediately jumped on it and added a second, third, and fourth job skill. They did that for another 3 years.

After this, they settled on a standard raise where every employee got the same amount of money at raise time based on how the company performed. But, some team members were working harder than others and contributing more. They decided to change the system to allow for those who were the higher contributors to actually get a bigger raise.

As they moved from system to system, it's important to know that it's complicated. It took a lot of time and effort. It required a lot of meetings and discussions with leadership and teams. And it evolves. As with any system, we need to respond to the challenge by asking, "Is this still meeting our needs? Is this still doing what we want it to do?"

17.6 SUMMARY

It should be clear at this point that engagement is a reciprocal relationship. A culture of employees who are highly engaged in their roles is the result of an organization that is highly engaged in its role. If an organization is not excited about its own purpose, how can the employees be excited about it? If an organization does not value the relationship between the employees and the organization itself, why would the employees value it? If an organization is not fostering and celebrating progress, how can employees be expected to get excited about it? A lack of purpose, value, and progress are the underlying problems that will result in the symptom of low levels of employee engagement. The organization needs to demonstrate its own high level of engagement if it expects to receive a similar high level of engagement from the employees. An organization that fosters a culture of purpose, value, and progress will enjoy the benefits of an excited, inspired, and highly engaged workforce.

> No company, small or large, can win over the long run without energized employees who believe in the mission and understand how to achieve it.
>
> **Jack Welch**

18

Onboarding

18.1 INTRODUCTION

Onboarding is the initiation or orientation process that organizations use to familiarize new employees and clients with the company. Starting a new job or working with a company for the first time can be a nerve-racking experience filled with anxiety and uncertainty. An effective onboarding process can help move past those initial anxious feelings and move on to more positive and productive feelings.

Many organizations don't take the time to develop and put into action an onboarding process for a variety of reasons. However, it is important to understand that the orientation process is happening with or without the organization's involvement. A formal onboarding program simply converts the orientation process from a painful experience into an exciting one.

So, why is a chapter about onboarding included in a book about strategy? For the execution of a strategy to be fully effective, every individual within the organization needs to be involved in supporting the strategy. Every individual needs to understand how he or she fits into the strategic plan. Additionally, because the strategy revolves around creating value for the client, every new client should be able to quickly understand how the organization's strategy will benefit them. The strategy must be cascaded throughout the organization, which includes new employees and new clients. Although there are many types of onboarding processes, in this chapter we discuss three main types. They are employee onboarding, executive onboarding, and client onboarding.

18.2 EMPLOYEE ONBOARDING

The most common type of onboarding is employee onboarding. As potential employees are recruited, they are typically given a sort of sales pitch promoting the organization. On the employee's first day of work, he or she is excited to be starting a great new opportunity with an exciting company. Unfortunately, that initial excitement often doesn't usually last long. The first day of work can become a day of confusion as the new employee spends the day enduring awkward encounters with existing employees, filling out new employee paperwork, and probably trying to look busy flipping through an employee handbook wondering what he or she is supposed to be doing.

Developing and consistently executing an effective employee onboarding process is a great way to take advantage of the enthusiasm brought into an organization by new employees. The employee onboarding process can convert the initial excitement into long-term employee engagement and can be used to initiate buy-in to the corporate strategy. It's also a great opportunity to introduce new employees to the culture of the organization and provide a clear understanding of expectations and opportunities. Think of the employee onboarding process as an opportunity to build new support for the corporate strategy and set the new employee up for long-term success.

The employee onboarding process should be formal and well organized. It should not be thought of as an event but rather a process that cannot be rushed. Someone in the organization should be selected to oversee the new employee onboarding process. The onboarding process should include a social aspect intended to help new employees build relationships quickly and initiate new employees into the culture. Although the employee onboarding process will be busy initially, it should slow down once the employee is engaged in his or her new role, and there should be monthly or quarterly check-ins for the first 6 months to a year. It should also include any necessary training or orientation and an introduction to the corporate strategy to build a clear understanding of where the organization is going. Additionally, each new employee should develop a personal development plan, and on a quarterly basis, managers should follow up with the employee regarding this plan.

Employee onboarding is a great way to reduce the turnover rate of an organization and initiate ownership of strategic objectives. Too often, organizations expect new employees to simply "get the hang of it" through time on the job. However, top talent will decide within the first 6 months if they are going to stay with the organization, and truly competitive organizations don't have the luxury of just hoping it works out. When an organization takes the time to execute an effective and consistent employee onboarding process, this demonstrates respect for the employees by treating them as allies, instead of treating them as servants. When employees are treated with respect, they will, in turn, share that respect with clients. When clients are treated with respect, revenues will increase, and the resources invested in the onboarding process will be returned to the organization many times over.

18.3 EXECUTIVE ONBOARDING

Bringing a new executive into an organization can be a very tense time. Staff are concerned about what changes the new executive will bring. They hope the changes will improve the culture of the organization and not complicate daily tasks. The tension, of course, is much warranted because a new executive can have a major impact on the organization and there can be a lot at stake. New executives tend to want to "make their mark" quickly and if they don't have the enterprise's strategic perspective in mind, their efforts can seriously harm what the organization wishes to accomplish. An effective executive onboarding process is critical to the facilitation of the executive's rapid assimilation into the organization.

An executive onboarding process needs to have a heavy focus on strategy. The existing corporate strategy should be clearly detailed, including the analysis that leads to its development, significant metrics, reporting methods, successes, and challenges. Additionally, the executive onboarding process should provide role alignment, an explanation of expectations, and a thorough introduction to the current business environment. The new executive needs to understand his or her role in achieving the enterprise's objectives. What is the "piece of the pie" that the executive has specifically been hired to accomplish? If an executive is not provided a thorough understanding of the existing conditions, his or her effectiveness could be significantly undermined.

The executive onboarding process should also focus on developing positive relationships between the new executive, key stakeholders, the other members of the executive team, and the rest of the employees. An executive who tries to initiate changes before developing relationships is more likely to experience significant resistance and may even inadvertently damage the culture of the organization and create disorder. To ensure cultural assimilation, follow-up surveys after 60 days of the executive's start date should be conducted. Surveys will not only provide the executive with valuable feedback but will also provide an opportunity for other members of the organization to contribute to the new executive's initiation into the organization.

Failing to carry out effective executive onboarding can potentially cost the organization dearly as the organization works to resist the new executive, instead of working to provide support. A strong executive onboarding process can quickly move the new executive through the initiation process and on to more significant contributions.

18.4 CLIENT ONBOARDING

Client onboarding is the process of welcoming and introducing a new client. This process is critical for establishing a great first impression and a rewarding customer experience. Organizations spend a great deal of time and resources attracting new clients. This investment means they really can't afford the new relationship to be damaged by a bad start. A poor first impression can have a significant impact on the organization's rapport with the client for the entire duration of the relationship, whereas a great first impression can lead to a rewarding and long-lasting relationship.

Client onboarding should provide a positive introduction to the organization and its service. The client should be clear about what services your organization offers and what makes your organization great at providing those services. Additionally, the client onboarding process should include introductions to key individuals that the new client will be interacting with on a regular basis. The client onboarding team also has the responsibility of gaining a thorough understanding of the client's needs and expectations. These needs and expectations should be recorded in an organized fashion so that those working with the client can reference and add to the client's needs and expectations as the new relationship develops further. This information should also be reviewed with the client at the beginning of every new project and should be included in the customer relationship management plan to ensure that a follow-up schedule is executed, thereby improving the customer experience over time.

Because attracting new clients can be a significant investment, retaining clients should be a top priority for every organization. Retaining clients starts with a great first impression and the development of a solid mutual understanding. A great start to a new relationship is more likely to lead to great customer experiences, which will then lead to obtaining more new clients by referral rather than by expensive marketing activities. Missing out on the chance to get the relationship off to a great start is not an opportunity that can be recovered later. Be sure to take advantage of the opportunity before it passes you by.

18.5 SUMMARY

Onboarding is an important and often overlooked aspect of effectively executing a corporate strategy. Through the effective onboarding of employees, executives, and clients, the corporate strategy is solidified and buy-in is renewed on a regular basis. The strategy becomes more apparent and more impactful as those new to the organization can quickly learn how it involves and affects them. The effectiveness of the strategy becomes diluted every time buy-in is not initiated through an effective onboarding process. Additionally, a great strategy that focuses on high performance and ideal behaviors creates a powerful culture. This requires new members to be quickly initiated into the culture, allowing them to feel and be accepted as part of the team. Through effective onboarding, your organization can create new enthusiasm for the strategy and ensure its longevity.

19

Communication

19.1 INTRODUCTION

During the NUMMI partnership, Toyota found that typical American parts manufacturers are good at selling their products but rarely get involved in the design stage of the end product, which they felt misses the mark when focusing on meeting customer requirements. Toyota introduced its concept of "design in" to involve parts suppliers in the design stage of the end product, which in the NUMMI case was the joint General Motors-Toyota car. Toyota engineers were called in from Japan to meet with local suppliers who were assembled at a hotel. They shared their strategy and initiated the joint development of certain automobile parts to enhance the synergy of working together. They created a level of communication between the customer (NUMMI) and the supplier, which was unheard of in the past in the United States.

In this chapter, we focus specifically on several key elements of communication as is relates to the corporate strategy. Effectively communicating the strategy is critical to effectively executing the strategy. A strategic plan lacking communication is nothing more than a very detailed wish that has no chance of actually becoming reality.

19.2 PURPOSE OF COMMUNICATION

Effective communication is critical to the success of any organization. Whether within the organization or outside the organization, establishing and maintaining clear lines of communication can greatly enhance all aspects of the organization and increase client satisfaction. Communication builds meaningful and long-lasting relationships and enhances those relationships over time. Although most managers would agree that communication is imperative, it seems to be one of those aspects of effective leadership that is common sense but not always common practice. Communication not only conveys information but also builds trusting relationships and enhances productivity. In terms of executing the strategy, a strategy that is not effectively communicated can never be effectively executed.

Through effective communication, organizations can develop a common understanding of the objectives, metrics, and all other aspects of the corporate strategy. This common understanding will help build strategic alignment and unity as organizational divisions work to achieve objectives. Communication can also make the strategy more applicable at all levels, enhance buy-in, and build enthusiasm. Clearly communicating the strategy also demonstrates the executive leadership team's dedication to the strategy. In addition to the importance of communication to the execution of the strategy, communication is critical to organizations in many other ways. Communication also improves collaboration, establishes unity, and facilitates effective teamwork. Improved collaboration then encourages innovation, creative thinking, and problem-solving. Organizations that maintain a focus on clear communication will also naturally develop an increase in transparency.

The difference between mere management and leadership is communication.

Winston Churchill

19.3 CHARACTERISTICS OF EFFECTIVE BUSINESS COMMUNICATION

Effective communication of the corporate strategy requires a communication plan that will not only present the plan but also make it relatable and build on the buy-in that was initiated during the strategic planning process. Communicating the strategy should not be thought of as an event but as an ongoing process. This process may begin with a kickoff event or a series of events to present the strategy; however, the majority of the work involved in communicating a strategy will happen after the kickoff event. Communicating the strategy should be happening on an ongoing basis through a variety of methods. Although visual reminders of the strategy can be helpful, a thorough communication plan should involve much more than just hanging a poster on the wall. It requires regular reinforcement of key aspects of the strategy and how it applies to each individual.

> The single biggest problem in communication is the illusion that it has taken place.
>
> **George Bernard Shaw**

Whether speaking with a staff member one-on-one, speaking to a large group, or writing a memo, there are many characteristics that make communication effective. When preparing a message, consider the attitudes and preconceptions of your audience, but also consider what is the best way to deliver the message. Who is the best person to deliver the message, and when and how often do we need to deliver the message. Take the time to consider what preparatory work needs to be done to eliminate barriers to the positive reception of your message. Deliver your message at a time when the message is more likely to be well received and the audience is not distracted or hurried. Communications should be confident, concise, to the point, and should include actionable information. It should be clear what the audience is expected to do with the message, i.e., what is their role in helping to achieve the strategy. Take the time to establish common ground and demonstrate the mutually beneficial purpose of alignment with the strategy. When speaking with small groups or one-on-one, always give the audience time to express opinions and use their concerns as opportunities to illustrate the strengths of the strategy in order to alleviate those concerns. Take the time to listen with the intention of developing understating.

> If you can't explain it simply, you don't understand it well enough.
>
> **Albert Einstein**

19.4 SUMMARY

Above all, keep communications positive and empowering. When discussing an issue, discuss it as an opportunity to learn and improve. Of course, communications need to be honest and realistic but there is always an opportunity in every problem. Innovation and forward momentum belong to those who can take advantage of the opportunities.

Phase IV

Refine: Stimulating Continuous Improvement through Cultural Vitality

20

Introduction to Refine

It is not necessary to change. Survival is not mandatory.

Dr. W. Edwards Deming

20.1 INTRODUCTION

In the Pharmaceutical Industry (pharma), we are plagued with an enormous amount of regulatory oversight, more than in any other industry. The Food and Drug Administration (FDA) can walk into a facility at any time and do an inspection, and the production facility must give them all the support and resources that they request, in labor, information, or any other resource. This is in addition to regularly scheduled inspections. Any deviation from the regulatory requirements can cause an immediate shutdown of the entire facility. Therefore, when a pharma production facility develops a strategy plan, it is filled with quality and regulatory expectations, and the entire facility becomes dependent on that strategy.

Within a pharma facility, there is an entire department focused on reliability engineering. This department describes itself as the team that focuses on maintaining the house after it's been built. It involves complex studies of equipment durability and reliability. It involves studies of each piece of equipment, making sure that any potential failures are recognized and prevented. It involves preventive maintenance and quick-response failure maintenance.

Within this reliability engineering program, we find all the characteristics that have been emphasized throughout this book. For example, standardization and standard work are critical. Clean work environments and 5S are critical. Data must be tracked and analyzed to dashboards and scorecards in a consistent manner. Software programs and reports must be standardized. The critical metrics are defined in the strategy and are closely monitored within the management systems. The costs of running a careful and thorough reliability engineering program are enormous but are considered insignificant when compared to losing weeks' or months' worth of production output because of a systems failure.

In a recent reliability report for a major pharma company that the author was working with, we find the quote, "Reliability is a culture and a way of thinking about assets that does not focus on failures, but rather, focuses on maintaining safety, environmental, and process Reliability." Even at the Reliability Engineering level, cultural development is prominent. The report goes on to say, "The culture of Life Asset Management is key to evaluating and understanding the design, application, risk, and cost throughout the life of the asset."

Strategically managing the culture of an organization is critical. This starts with a uniform and understandable strategic plan and the plan needs to be filtered down through all levels of an organization. However, no matter how good the plan is today, it will need to be updated and refined in the future, and that's where continuous improvement and the "Refine" stage of strategy development becomes a necessary element.

The final phase of Strategic Excellence is the Refine phase. Once a strategy has been developed and executed, the work of strategic management continues. Strategy is not an event, it's an ongoing process carefully integrated with the culture of the organization. The Refine phase in this book focuses primarily on solving problems using the strategic methodology and maintaining continuous improvement.

> Unless someone like you cares a whole awful lot, nothing is going to get better. It's not.
>
> **Dr. Seuss**

20.2 WHY REFINE?

The Refine phase will maintain the momentum that was initiated during the Analyze, Define, and Execute phases. It will also reinforce enterprise alignment and organization-wide ownership of the strategy. As the executive team keeps the pressure on the strategy, their dedication to it will be made evident to the organization and the employees will understand that the corporate strategy is not something that will blow over in a couple of months. Most strategies will ultimately fail because the organizations fail to establish a continued commitment to them. The Refine phase can be a fantastic opportunity for organizations to build excitement for the strategy. As the organization begins to see strategic success, take some time to celebrate the success. Also, take every opportunity to point out evidence of the benefits of the established governing principles. Remember: The principles discussed in this book are results oriented. That means that if the organization is true to the principles established, then the beneficial results will be evident. The Refine phase is executed using problem-solving tools along with the establishment of a culture of continuous improvement.

It's common practice in the AEC industry for the leading technical experts to be promoted into positions of management. However, many of those technical experts have never been trained to deal with business problems. As a result, many managers in the AEC industry, when faced with a business problem, will often ignore the problem and hope that it resolves itself. This is not because the manager doesn't care. It's because the manager doesn't know how to approach a business problem. Learning some of the effective tools and techniques for problem solving in a business setting will allow the manager to feel more comfortable addressing the problems, rather than ignoring them. Additionally, the problem-solving tools and techniques presented in the Refine phase should be taught to the staff members involved in the process of solving problems.

Solving problems in a business setting can be a challenge for technical experts. They're used to developing solutions to technical problems which result in one final answer. In a business setting, there are often many possible tools and methods that can be used to solve problems. The manager is responsible for helping his or her team determine the best tools and methods to be used in the search for an effective solution. The Refine phase presents several problem-solving tools and techniques to assist the problem-solving team as they work to develop the best solution for their specific situation.

Although solving problems is a major aspect of the Refine phase, it is only the beginning. Long-term, sustainable Strategic Excellence and continuous improvement require a vibrant culture of strategic thinking and innovation. Your strategy will never survive in the long-run if it is not linked to a vibrant culture.

CHART 20.1
Strategic Excellence Model – Refine Phase.

20.3 APPROACH TO REFINE

The general approach to refine is simple: Solve the problems and keep improving. However, how that is accomplished can take a significant amount of effort. And it should, considering the valuable benefits that can result. Most organizations in the AEC industry will face the same types of problems. If you and your organization can resolve them, your organization will have a significant competitive advantage.

In the Refine phase, as we have in the other phases, we will emphasize the importance of culture in this process. Your strategy will never survive without a strong continuous improvement and enterprise excellence-focused culture. The above image outlines the Refine phase (Chart 20.1).

20.4 SUMMARY

The Refine phase can be the difference between a strategy that is just another attempt to make a difference and a strategy that drives long-term continuous improvement. The Refine phase is what makes a strategic plan sustainable. Although the Refine phase can take significant effort, it can also be very exciting because this is when major improvements can be enjoyed. Remember: The long-term success of your strategy will be dependent on the organization's culture. A healthy and vibrant culture does not happen on its own, it must be intentionally created. Create a culture that empowers every employee to make improvements, and then continuous improvement will happen naturally.

> These people are very smart. They're not pawns. They're very smart. And if given the opportunity to change and improve, they will. They will improve the processes if there's a mechanism for it.

Steve Jobs

21

Problem Solving

21.1 INTRODUCTION

Solving problems using root cause analysis is possible by using a two-step methodology. The first step is to seek the true root cause by repeatedly asking the question why. The second step is to ask questions about the object's purpose by using the purpose expansion. Both Sakichi Toyoda and Kiichiro Toyoda provided the critical thought process that was needed. Accordingly, they were able to think through and identify the specific purposes. Automobile engineers are normally focused only on the production of cars, but Kiichiro's thought process was different. As he stated, his purpose was "not the assembly of cars but rather to promote the automobile industry throughout Japan." Before solving a specific problem, he asked engineers to review the purpose of solving the problem and if that purpose doesn't support the goals and strategies of the organization, then why solve the problem? His thought process and his insights were extremely unique for business development in his day.

The application of advanced understanding and useful tools to solve challenging problems is the fundamental purpose of the Architectural, Engineering, and Construction (AEC) industry. Through education, training, and experience, AEC professionals become very good at solving AEC problems. Unfortunately, an ability to solve AEC problems does not naturally translate into an ability to solve business-related problems, and as a result, many AEC leaders seem to avoid dealing with the business problems. The solving of business-related problems requires additional understanding and tools, a few of which will be discussed in this chapter.

> Most people spend more time and energy going around problems than in trying to solve them.
>
> **Henry Ford**

Additionally, solving problems in an organization cannot be the responsibility of one or a few. Effectively solving the problems of the organization requires a problem-solving culture. Problems will come up at all levels of the organization and in every operational unit. For this reason, it is essential that problem-solving skills be developed throughout the organization so that every member of the organization has the ability to solve the problems related to his or her job function.

Establishing a culture of problem solving requires that all members of the organization be trained with the necessary problem-solving methodologies and tools and that all members of the organization be empowered with the authority to solve the problems relating to their own job function and mentored and supported in their efforts to do so. Let's discuss a few of the major problem-solving methodologies. These methodologies are designed to help you and your organization drill down to the root cause of the problem, so that you don't waste time just treating the symptoms. They will also help you to focus on fixing the systems that created the problem, instead of trying to find an individual to blame for it.

21.2 DMAIC

DMAIC is a Six Sigma structured methodology used to solve problems and improve the efficiency of an organization's processes. Used regularly, it can help create a culture of continuous improvement. DMAIC stands for Define, Measure, Analyze, Improve, and Control. The DMAIC process can be facilitated by many Six Sigma tools, many of which are listed in Chapter 22 of this book (Chart 21.1).

21.2.1 Define

The Define stage consists of creating a project charter that clearly outlines what the problem is. The project charter should also include information about the project team and any resources that may be needed to develop

CHART 21.1
DMAIC process.

solutions. Additionally, the Define stage should identify and detail the voice of the customer to promote solutions that add value for the customer.

21.2.2 Measure

The Measure stage consists of developing measurements to better understand the magnitude of the problem. The measurement will continue throughout the project to track progress and make adjustments as needed.

21.2.3 Analyze

The Analyze stage focuses on getting to the root cause of the problem. This stage requires taking the time to ask many questions to ensure that the solutions developed are long-lasting solutions that will add value to the customer and not just be a quick relief from symptoms.

21.2.4 Improve

The Improve stage develops ways to solve the problem. It requires a focus on the root cause of the problem and attention to the voice of the customer. As solutions are implemented, the established measures should be monitored to ensure that the solutions are producing the desired results.

21.2.5 Control

The Control stage focuses on continuing to measure the progress of the solutions set in place. It also requires that effective solutions be made a standard part of the system to maintain progress.

21.3 A3

A3 is a Lean problem-solving methodology that can assist in removing waste and establishing continuous improvements throughout the organization. The A3 is a control tool that can be used to track and report on the progress of any project from start to finish. Although there are many different approaches to the A3 process, this book recommends an 8-step approach. Steps 1 and 2 focus on defining the problem in depth. Steps 3 through 5 focus on developing a solution that addresses the root cause of the problem. Steps 6 and 7 establish measurements to track improvements and step 8 focuses on distributing the lessons learned. The following image is adapted from the book, *Driving Strategy to Execution using Lean Six Sigma*, which provides additional information about each step of the process (Plenert and Cluley, 2012). There are several Lean tools listed in Chapter 22 of this book that can be used to facilitate the A3 process (Chart 21.2).

Team members: Who are the individuals who worked on this 8-step report?	**8-Step opportunity (problem) analysis tool**	**Approval information/signatures:** Who are the champions for (signers of) this project?
1. Clarify and validate the problem: State the basic overall fundamental problem that needs to be solved and validate that it is strategically aligned with the enterprise objectives.	**4. Determine root causes:** Define the root-causes of the current problem and the reason for the current performance gaps. What caused the need for this project?	**6. Execute improvement tasks:** Prioritize the actions listed in step 5, time sequence them, identify specific completion dates, assign responsibility for the completion, and state where help is needed in order to complete the action. What are the deliverables and their dates?
2. Break down the problem/identify performance gaps: What are the facts? List what specifically needs to change to solve the problem and what are the performance gaps to be closed to realize required performance. Prove it!	**5. Develop improvement task list:** List the specific actions that need to be implemented to create change and close performance gaps. Validate that all the root causes listed in step 4 have been accounted for and resolved. What needs to change in order to eliminate the root cause?	**7. Confirm results:** Report progress made on the improvement targets listed in step 3. Confirm that we are doing the right things in the right way by improving the desired performance areas. Did you achieve your desired results? (At-a-glance status)
3. Set improvement targets: Set improvement targets. Identify annual and long term stretch targets as appropriate.		**8. Standardize successful processes:** List ways to institutionalize best practices learned from implementing this change. How can we institutionalize this "best practice"?

CHART 21.2
8-Step A3 problem-solving.

21.4 KAIZEN/LEAN/RAPID IMPROVEMENT EVENT

Kaizen is a Toyota Production System (TPS) problem-solving methodology (also referred to as the Lean Event or the RIE – Rapid Improvement Event) used to create a problem-solving culture that engages every member of the organization in an effort to solve problems at the source. The Kaizen methodology sees every aspect of the organization as an opportunity to improve. Each member of the organization is encouraged to contribute ideas for improvements. By involving every employee, a culture of continuous improvement is established, resulting in improvements throughout all levels of the organization. This approach also encourages regular small improvements throughout the organization, which add up to significant improvements.

The Kaizen approach to problem solving can include Kaizen Events, which are short-term events, usually one week or less, that focus efforts on rapidly solving a problem or improving a process. The Kaizen Event typically has a facilitator but should include the individuals who work in the area where the problem exists. There are several TPS tools listed in Chapter 22 that can be used to facilitate the Kaizen process (Chart 21.3).

21.4.1 Orientation

The Orientation stage focuses on defining and documenting the current state. Tools that may be useful at this stage are value stream mapping and defining the voice of the customer.

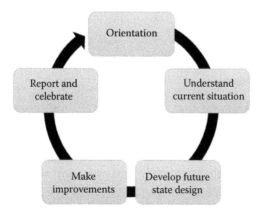

CHART 21.3
Kaizen.

21.4.2 Understand the Problem

Understanding the problem requires a cause-and-effect analysis that will drill down to the root of the problem and identify bottlenecks. Tools that may help with this stage are Ishikawa Diagram and the five Whys.

21.4.3 Develop Future State Design

Developing the Future State Design involves characterizing the ideal future state of the process being analyzed and documenting the wastes that need to be eliminated. The typical wastes of organizations in the service industry include defects, overproduction, overprocessing or overanalyzing, transportation of materials or information, the unnecessary motion of employees, waiting, underutilized staff, and too much inventory.

21.4.4 Make the Improvements

Making the Improvements stage involves creating a list of action items that need to be accomplished (see Step 5 in Chart 21.2), defining a schedule for the execution of each of the steps, and then proceeding with implementing the improvements. The most common tool for making improvements is the A3, Standard Work, and 5S.

21.4.5 Report and Celebrate

The Report and Celebrate stage focuses on standardizing improvements and sharing the lessons learned. It also involves celebrating the success of the Kaizen Event.

21.5 SUMMARY

Problem-solving begins with asking the right questions to fully understand the root cause of the problem and then implementing the solution that will be most likely to simplify processes, add value to the customer, and empower employees. Your greatest asset in any problem-solving situation is not the manager in his corner office, it's the employees who have developed an intimate understanding of the problem because they've been fighting it toe-to-toe. If you do not take advantage of their enlightened perspective, you will never be able to discover the ideal solution.

As problems are solved, remember to focus on solutions that simplify processes. Complexity will only breed more problems and more waste. Solutions should always be aligned with the enterprise strategy in the sense that solving problems and improving processes should be prioritized based on strategic objectives. Never lose sight of the voice of the customer. If an improvement does not add value to the customer, then it is a waste, not an improvement. Adding a control point or check mechanism is not an improvement. It's just an added step to the system. Fix the overall system that is causing the failure. Continuous improvement requires a problem-solving culture that breaks down silos and increases transparency. Don't avoid problems, embrace them until the problems are so well understood that the solutions are obvious.

It's not that I'm so smart, it's just that I stay with problems longer.

Albert Einstein

22

Lean, Six Sigma and TPS

People who are satisfied with the way things are can never achieve improvement or progress.

Shigeo Shingo
The Sayings of Shigeo Shingo, p. 17

22.1 INTRODUCTION

In business, as in construction, there is no universal tool that can be used to accomplish any and all tasks. Different situations require different tools and the more tools you are familiar with and skilled at using, the more situations you will be prepared to confront. In this chapter, we focus on presenting many useful tools that can be used to solve problems and promote continuous improvement.

The author was involved in a lean project for a pharmaceutical company. They needed to increase the capacity of their pill production facility and they were searching to acquire additional equipment. The author did a quick survey of the process and quickly identified that the process contained about 10 steps and that one of the steps was the bottleneck. This bottleneck was at the compression presses. Taking a closer look at the presses and breaking down their operation, it was discovered that the tear-down/clean-up/set-up time for the presses was anywhere from 30 to 40 hours, depending on who was doing the set-up. The actual run time for the presses, where they were compressing pills, was about 4 hours. The author suggested to the facility leadership that, rather than purchase additional presses, they should use Lean to reduce the tear-down/clean-up/set-up time. If this could be cut in half, then they would have been able to double capacity on the existing equipment. Leadership was skeptical, but they allowed the author to proceed.

The press equipment ran on four different machines, 24 hours a day (three shifts), and each of the machines had a team of two to three employees operating the equipment. This meant that there were 12 teams, or around 30 employees, each with his or her own version of how the tear-down/clean-up/set-up should run. The first thing that had to happen was that a standard work methodology had to be created, which would be followed by all the teams. To do this, a Rapid Improvement Event (RIE) had to be run where representatives from most of the teams came in and diagrammed their process on a Value Stream Map (VSM). It's interesting to note that during the mapping process, several redundancies and overlaps were identified because the cleaning process crossed several shifts. Also, some missing steps and gaps in the tear-down/clean-up/set-up were identified, which caused leadership some concern because the Food and Drug Administration could close their shop if they knew about these failures.

The VSM exercise mapped out and created a standard work, and a large standard work checklist sheet was created and posted in each of the press rooms. The employees could now follow a consistent process. Each team knew what had already been completed by the previous shift and what needed to be done next.

This standard process was used by all teams for about 1 month to confirm that this was a workable standard. What was discovered was that the tooling necessary to do the process wasn't always readily available. Teams were stealing tools from each other because there wasn't the correct amount of tooling available for each press. This would cause delays in the clean-up. The author had the teams perform a 5S exercise where they created shadow boxes for each of the presses, and each shadow box contained the toolset necessary to perform the tear-down/clean-up/set-up process for that press. Using shadow boxes made it easy to identify if a tool was missing, and discipline had to be incorporated which required each tool to be returned to the shadow box when the tool was no longer needed.

The creation of standard work, the cleanup with 5S, and tools like VSM and Shadow Boxes were all necessary before a reasonable effort could be made to reduce the cycle time of the tear-down/clean-up/set-up process. This total effort took several months, and at this point, the average cycle time was about 34 hours. The Lean RIE team could now be reconvened with a focus on cycle time reduction. They discovered that a lot of the processes that were being done in the press room could be performed outside of the press room during the run. They discovered that by adding an extra individual to each team, this third individual could be doing work outside of the press room that this would reduce the work that was occurring in the press room and was currently adding to the cycle time. This required an extra employee, but it was significantly cheaper than acquiring additional equipment and requiring additional teams of employees to run that equipment.

Numerous changes were made to the process, including sequencing (which step was performed when), changes in some of the tooling, quicker access to cleaning equipment, etc. In the end, the cycle time for the tear-down/clean-up/set-up was reduced from the 34-hour average down to an unbelievable 2 hours. Most of the 34-hour effort was deemed waste because it involved moving, storing, sorting, etc. which could be accomplished by creating shadow boxes for the press parts as they were being cleaned. Enormous waste steps were eliminated. Capacity was increased to the point where they had excess capacity. And no additional presses were acquired. Compression was no longer the bottleneck. It had now moved to the mixing process, which took longer than the presses. The cost of the change included incorporating an additional team member to each team, and creating some shadow boxes and cleaning cages.

The point of this story is to stress that there is not one magic button that will fix all the problems. Big changes are possible, but they take time, knowing which tool to use and when, and several iterations of effort.

22.2 LEAN

The Lean methodology is one of the Toyota Production System (TPS) tools which focuses on eliminating waste within processes or systems. Every process has a certain amount of waste and the cost of that waste is paid for by the customer. For example, when you purchase a candy bar, what you want is the candy bar. However, you not only pay for the candy bar, you also pay for the wrapper and all the design and manufacturing work that was involved in producing it. You also pay for warehousing and transportation costs, the costs associated with repairing faulty manufacturing equipment including the employee downtime while the machinery is being repaired. You pay for all the television ads, radio ads, and other types of marketing costs, including all the employees dedicated to managing the marketing campaigns. Let's say you pay $1.00 for the candy bar, how much does the actual materials of the candy bar cost? You can quickly see that the majority of what you're paying for is not actually the candy bar itself, but all the additional associated costs. All those additional costs are waste. Anything that does not add direct value to the client, or in other words, anything that the client didn't necessarily want to pay for, is waste.

Every process will have some level of waste that cannot be eliminated. However, most goods and services are provided through processes that are riddled with nonvalue-adding waste. I would argue that the service industry has more waste than most other industries. And of the services industry, the Architectural, Engineering, and Construction (AEC) industry has probably one of the highest levels of all.

Right now, you should be thinking that this is great news! Why? Because waste is a big problem for the AEC industry. If it's a big problem, then it's a big opportunity! Any organization in the AEC industry that takes the time to start eliminating waste and making their processes more lean and efficient will find themselves in a highly competitive position. They will be able to provide better service through a faster response time at more competitive pricing and retain more of the revenue as profit.

The Lean approach to improving processes includes several useful tools. The following figure (Chart 22.1) lists a number of these tools, several of which will be briefly introduced in this section. Remember that these are just tools and none of them should be thought of as some golden solution to all your problems.

Lean Tools		
5S	Kaizen	Replenishment pull
Analytical batch sizing	Kanban	Root cause analysis
Andon	Line balancing	Sales and operational planning
Bottleneck analysis	Mistake-proofing	Setup reduction
Constraint identification	Muda	Six big losses
Continuous flow	Non-value-added analysis	Standardized work
Gemba	PDCA	Takt time
Generic pull	Poka-yoke	Time trap analysis
Heijunka	Process cycle efficiency	TPM
Hoshin Kanri	Process flow improvement	Value stream map
Jidoka	Process sizing	Visual factory
Just-in-time	Queuing theory	Visual process control

CHART 22.1
Lean Tools.

22.2.1 5S

5S is a Lean tool used to organize the workplace to increase productivity and reduce the amount of time and resources wasted in dealing with unorganized tools, materials, and workstations or desks. Each S of the 5S system is described as follows:

1. *Sort* work areas in order to simplify workflow by removing unnecessary tools and materials.
2. *Set in Order* all necessary tools and materials to make them easy to find and ready to use when needed.
3. *Shine* or clean the workplace on a regular basis to keep everything in its place and prevent clutter.
4. *Standardize* all processes and expectations to increase speed and efficiency of workflow.
5. *Sustain* processes by establishing discipline through training and effective communication.

22.2.2 Bottleneck Analysis

A bottleneck is any step in a process where a relative decrease in the speed of production is caused by a congestion in workflow. Bottlenecks in an AEC process can result in schedule delays, causing frustration and potential lawsuits. Bottlenecks can also reduce the amount of work an AEC organization can complete because the speed of production at the bottleneck will limit the overall production capacity. The throughput of a process is no faster than its slowest step, and that step is the bottleneck. Bottleneck analysis is used to identify current bottlenecks in order to identify potential opportunities to correct them. The following image (Chart 22.2) illustrates a general bottleneck analysis of a design process, which identifies a bottleneck at the review stage, and then illustrates the process with the bottleneck removed.

22.2.3 Visual Process Control

Visual Process Control is a Lean technique used to make different stages of a process clearly visual. It allows the progress of projects to be clearly and quickly communicated and reduces the amount of time that workers spend running around the office or the job site trying to find out what

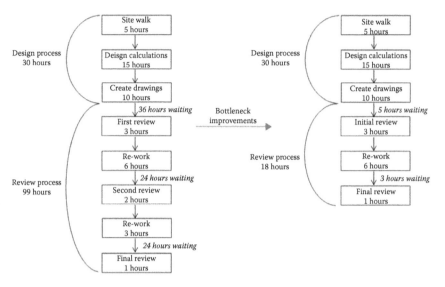

CHART 22.2
Bottleneck analysis.

needs to be done next or where the team is at in the process. It makes communication more obvious and easier by employing simple visual signals, rather than using written messages or at times a complete lack of communication altogether.

22.2.4 PDCA

PDCA is a Lean process improvement tool for stepping through the improvement process using a scientific approach. PDCA stands for Plan-Do-Check-Act. The Plan step is used to define the desired outcomes of the proposed process improvement. The Do step sets the plan into action and measures the resulting changes in process outcomes. The Check step compares the desired outcomes from the Plan step to the actual outcomes from the Do step to determine if the proposed improvement is an appropriate and complete solution correcting the "big picture" and not just a symptom. The Act phase either sets the proposed improvement as the new standard or maintains the existing process. The PDCA tool is used in iterations to test proposed improvements and determine if they should be standardized. The following image (Chart 22.3) shows a typical PDCA iteration.

CHART 22.3
PDCA process.

22.2.5 Six Big Losses

The Six Big Losses are the main areas where waste can typically be found. Thinking about your organization in terms of these six areas can help you identify how to improve. The following is a list of the Six Big Losses along with an explanation of each loss:

1. Breakdowns – This is demonstrated in the example at the start of Chapter 20 where we discussed Reliability Engineering. The cost of a breakdown in the system is often significantly more expensive than the cost of preventive maintenance.
2. Setup and Adjustments – This can be seen in the example of the setup costs of the fender preparation machine in Section 4.3 of Chapter 4. The waste of nonoptimized setups can be seen in the unnecessary inventory costs it creates.
3. Small Stops and Idling – This occurs when a process or system is constantly and is unnecessarily interrupted. When a product is not being worked on, then the gap time is waste.
4. Speed Losses – This occurs when we rush to get something done and because of the rush, we make mistakes.
5. Production Defects – This occurs when quality is not as important as throughput. Employees who are measured by throughput will continue to produce, and let someone else work on the quality issues. The story at the start of Chapter 12 exemplifies this failure.
6. Start-Up Rejects – This occurs because there is no standard work for the setup process. Everyone does the setup differently and it becomes a trial-and-error process before the setup is correct. The rejects from this start-up and the time wasted going through the random setup process are the waste.

22.2.6 Standardized Work

Standardized work is the act of defining the processes used and the time each process should take. The basic problem is that in most companies, they define what needs to be done but not how it should be done. This results in numerous employees each doing the process in their own way. Then, when we want to search for improvements to the process, it's impossible to make any improvements unless you look for improvements to each of the different ways of doing the process. If the process becomes standardized, then it's easier to make standard improvements, which will affect everyone across the board.

Standard work includes defining the standard process, defining the time for each step in the process, and the tools or resources needed to complete each step. Setting a standard encourages work to be completed in an efficient and consistent manner. It also establishes a baseline for any potential future improvements to be compared to. Standardized work is a highly effective yet much underutilized Lean tool.

22.3 SIX SIGMA

The Six Sigma methodology focuses on variability, which is consistent with establishing high quality. It involves the application of a research and data-driven approach to achieving near perfect quality. Six Sigma tools are used to eliminate variations in the product or service being provided to deliver a consistent high-quality experience for every customer. The following figure (Chart 22.4) lists many Six Sigma tools, several of which are explained following the list.

22.3.1 Five Whys

The Five Whys tool is a TPS interrogative approach used in both Lean and Six Sigma to determine the root cause of a problem. It involves asking the question "why" multiple times to arrive at the true source of a defect. Typically, the question "why" is asked five times, but the concept is to keep asking "why" until the cause of the mistake is fully understood. The following is an example of the Five Whys applied to a defect on a construction site. In this example, it may initially seem that the framers have failed to perform their jobs correctly and may need to be reprimanded. However,

Six sigma tools		
5 whys	High-level process map	Project charter
Affinity diagram	Histogram	Project commissioning
Analysis of variance (ANOVA)	House of quality	Project replication
Analytic hierarchy process (AHP)	Hypothesis testing	Project selection tools
Basic statistical tools	Impelementation plan	Pugh matrix
Benchmarking	Ishikawa diagram	QFD
Box plot	Kanban	RACI diagram
Brainstorming	Kano analysis	Simple and multiple regressions
C & E matrix	Measurement system analysis	SIPOC map
Communication plan	Multi-generation plan	Solutions selections matrix
Confidence intervals	Operational definitions	SOP
Control charts	Pareto chart	Stakeholder analysis
Data collection plan	Piloting and simulation	Statistical sampling
Design of experiments (DOE)	PIP management process	Surveys
Detailed 'as-is' process maps	Plan-do-check-act (PDCA)	'To-be' process maps
Financial analysis	Process capability	Training plan
FMEA	Process control plans	VOC and Kano analysis

CHART 22.4
Six Sigma tools.

after completing the Five Whys, it can be seen that the defect is not the fault of the framers. By completing the Five Whys, the root cause of a defect can be determined to develop a more effective solution. It is used to find and fix the root cause of the problem, not just the symptom.

Defect: The wood framing of a new building is complete but did not pass inspection.

1. Why did it not pass inspection?
   Answer – Because the nailing of the wood diaphragm sheathing is defective.
2. Why is the nailing defective?
   Answer – Because many of the nails are driven too deep.
3. Why were the nails driven so deep?
   Answer – Because some of the company's nail guns drive them too deep.
4. Why do some of the nail guns drive nails too deep?
   Answer – Because some of them are old and the depth adjustments are broken, causing the nails to be driven at inconsistent depths.
5. Why have the broken nail guns not been replaced?
   Answer – The framers have asked for new guns, but their request continues to be denied.

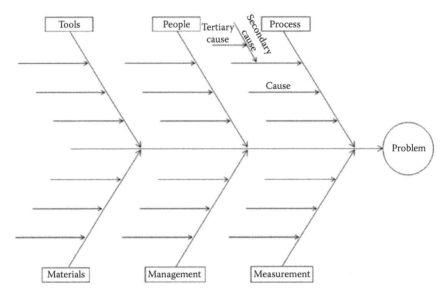

CHART 22.5
Ishikawa Diagram.

22.3.2 Ishikawa Diagram

The Ishikawa Diagram, also known as the fishbone diagram, is a visual representation of the root causes of a problem. It is another tool that we used to drill down to the root cause of a problem. It's a great way to clearly organize a group discussion that analyzes the cause and effect relationships that are contributing to some issues in need of improvement. The above figure (Chart 22.5) illustrates the general elements of an Ishikawa Diagram.

22.3.3 Project Charter

A Project Charter is used to detail the purpose and extent of improvement projects. It defines responsibility and ownership of the project. It focuses the efforts of all the members of the project team by clearly defining project limits. The Project Charter helps prevent the team from drifting off course and wasting time pursuing irrelevant avenues. A Project Charter typically consists of the following information:

- Problem Statement – A clear description of what the problem is that the improvement project is intended to resolve.
- Project Team – The key individuals who will be participating in the improvement project.

- Business Case – A convincing description of how the improvement project will improve operations and add value to the client or customer.
- Goals – Well-defined SMART goal(s) the improvement project will work to achieve.
- Measurements – Well-defined set of measurements that will identify the progress of the improvement project.
- Scope and Time Line – A clearly defined scope of work including an explanation of what the project is, what it isn't, and how long it will take.

22.3.4 VOC and Kano Analysis

VOC stands for the Voice of Customer, which is the process of gaining a thorough understanding of what the customer wants. The VOC can be developed through customer interviews, surveys, direct observation, or other forms of customer feedback. Once the VOC is well understood, it can be used to develop a Kano Analysis, which is a tool used to prioritize the characteristics of a product or service being offered based on the VOC. The product or service characteristics are located on a graph based on the following three major criteria:

- Basic – These are the characteristics that the customer is expecting to be present without having to say so. They are the characteristics that must be included in the product or services to meet the minimum acceptable standards.
- Performance – These are the characteristics that the customer hopes for. They are the characteristics that, when present, would make the customer consider your firm to be a relatively higher-performing firm.
- Delight – These are the characteristics that the customer would be pleasantly surprised to discover. They are the characteristics that would make the customer see your firm as one that goes above and beyond to deliver an exceptional product or service.

This process needs to be reviewed annually, working directly with the customer. There are numerous examples of why this is important. For example, 10 years ago, the car airbag would have fallen into the Delight category but today it falls into the Basic category. Customer expectations are a moving target and what is true today will not be true in the future.

The following figure (Chart 22.6) illustrates a basic Kano Analysis based on the VOC. The vertical axis is the level of customer satisfaction. The horizontal axis is the level of achievement. The bottom curved line represents the characteristics that are considered Basic. The diagonal line represents the characteristics that are considered Performance. The top curved line represents characteristics that are considered Delight. A few general characteristics are located appropriately on the graph. Keep in mind that your Kano Analysis must be customized based on the VOC. Do not assume you know what matters most to the customer until the customer has told you.

22.4 TPS

The Toyota Production System (TPS) is a cultural approach to Lean and is the original source of Lean and Six Sigma tools and concepts. While modern practitioners of Lean seem to focus on using tools to remove waste even if it hurts the culture of the organization, TPS focuses on developing a powerful Lean culture of productive individuals who use Lean tools to improve processes and enhance culture concurrently. While Lean and Six Sigma tools can be powerful agents in continuous improvement efforts, without a vibrant supporting culture they will never be able to reach their full potential. True organizational transformation requires the development of a healthy and empowering culture. It is the cultural approach to Lean that produces long-lasting continuous improvement, rather than short bursts of segmented improvements.

> The key to the Toyota Way and what makes Toyota stand out is not any of the individual elements – but what is important is having all of the elements together as a system. It must be practiced every day in a very consistent manner, not in spurts.
>
> **Taiichi Ohno**

TPS incorporates many powerful principles, all of which can be found in the book, *The Toyota Way*, by Jeffrey K. Liker (Liker, 2004). A few of the principles found in The Toyota Way are quoted as follows:

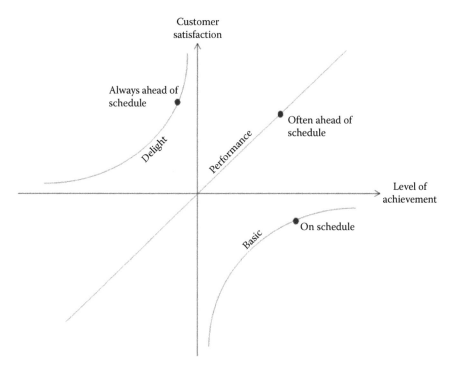

CHART 22.6
Kano Analysis.

- "Base your management decisions on a long-term philosophy, even at the expense of short-term financial goals."
- "Build a culture of stopping to fix problems, to get quality right the first time."
- "Standardized tasks and processes are the foundation for continuous improvement and employee empowerment."
- "Use visual controls so no problems are hidden."
- "Grow leaders who thoroughly understand the work, live the philosophy, and teach it to others."
- "Develop exceptional people and teams who follow your company's philosophy."
- "Go and see for yourself to thoroughly understand the situation."
- "Make decisions slowly by consensus, thoroughly considering all options; implement decisions rapidly."
- "Become a learning organization through relentless reflection and continuous improvement."

22.5 SUMMARY

It is common for technical experts to get in the habit of employing their favorite handful of tools and lose sight of the big picture. Especially in the West (USA and Europe), we focus on finding the one quick fix that will solve everything. We latch onto one tool, like quality circles, or Six Sigma, and think we now have the magic formula that will make us successful. Remember that Lean and Six Sigma tools are simply that, tools. A hammer is a very productive tool, but if used incorrectly, it can cause significant damage. Similarly, swinging a hammer without a blueprint or a clear understanding of the objective can be a very exhausting and pointless endeavor. Lean and Six Sigma tools can be very productive but should always be applied correctly and with strategic objectives in mind. Take the time to learn not only how to use the tools but also when to use the tools. And always use them in a supportive role meant to enhance a culture of continuous improvement.

23

Shingo

When I began visiting companies and production plants, there was one thing I almost always used to tell company presidents, 'The medicine I am prescribing for you is a miracle drug and very powerful, but there is one problem with it.'

'What problem?' they would say.

'The problem,' I would explain, 'is that the medicine won't work unless you take it. I may tell you wonderful things, but you're not going to be successful unless you actually do what I'm telling you.'

The Sayings of Shigeo Shingo, p. 160

23.1 INTRODUCTION

Countless organizations have dedicated significant resources to the application of one continuous improvement tool after another only to experience short bursts of improvements, rather than long-term, ongoing, sustainable improvement. Those within the organization who have been involved in the improvement efforts often become frustrated and burn out quickly because every improvement they make seems to produce only limited results. Bad habits always seem to creep back into the organization, no matter how many times you chase them away. Not only that, but improvement efforts typically seem to be focused on only one problem or one organizational unit while ignoring and sometimes hurting other aspects of the organization.

The Shingo approach to continuous improvement is not a tool or list of tools but it returns to the original Toyota Production Systems (TPS) approach, which was heavily focused on the cultural approach to establishing momentum towards enterprise excellence. It works to drive ideal results by focusing on ideal behaviors founded in a set of governing principles. Rather than only focusing on tools, it focuses on culture and allows the organizations the flexibility of using appropriate tools that support the cultural foundation. It is by first establishing a healthy and dynamic culture of continuous improvement that sustainable momentum towards excellence can be achieved.

The Shingo Model recognizes that tools are only half of the formula for creating an enterprise excellence model focused on continuous improvement. The other half, which makes this enterprise excellence model successful, is the critical cultural shift. By identifying culture-based principles that are universal, and by making these principles part of the enterprise's strategy, the necessary cultural shift can be achieved. This makes the continuous improvement mentality universal, rather than just a one-hit wonder.

23.2 THE SHINGO INSTITUTE

The Shingo Institute was established in 1988 by Utah State University and is named after Shigeo Shingo. Although the institute began as just the Shingo Prize, it has expanded its mission to provide various educational opportunities at Utah State University and through a worldwide network of affiliates.

Shigeo Shingo was one of the primary contributors to TPS and worked closely with Toyota executives, such as Taiichi Ohno, in the development of Lean tools and principles. Shingo dedicated his life to the enhancement of the Lean principles and spent years consulting for numerous companies and providing training throughout Japan and the United States. Shingo wrote 17 books, eight of which have been translated into English.

The Shingo Prize, initiated in 1988, was established to recognize organizations that have achieved high levels of operational excellence. Over time, the Shingo Prize evolved into the Shingo Institute, which now offers workshops, conferences, and study tours through licensed affiliates and certified facilitators spread throughout the world. The Shingo Prize, which now focuses not only on operational excellence but also enterprise excellence as a whole, has expanded to offer a Shingo Research Award and a Shingo Publication Award.

The Shingo workshops are a series of five workshops held over 2–3 days that combine in-class instruction with on-site observation. The workshops are held at host organizations worldwide and are conducted by experienced facilitators trained specifically in the Shingo Model. The five Shingo workshops are outlined as follows:

1. Discover Excellence – This is the introductory workshop that acts as a prerequisite to all other workshops. It introduces The Shingo Model, The Shingo Guiding Principles, and the Three Insights of Enterprise Excellence.
2. Cultural Enablers – This workshop focuses on the Guiding Principles associated with Cultural Enablers which are Respect Every Individual and Lead with Humility.
3. Continuous Improvement – This workshop focuses on the Guiding Principles associated with Continuous Improvement, which are Seek Perfection, Embrace Scientific Thinking, Focus on Process, Ensure Quality at the Source, and Flow and Pull Value.
4. Enterprise Alignment and Results – This workshop focuses on the Guiding Principles associated with Enterprise Alignment and Results, which are Think Systematically, Create Constancy of Purpose, and Create Value for the Customer.
5. Build Excellence – This workshop is the capstone workshop which focuses on creating a plan for the execution of the principles established in the other workshops.

23.3 THE SHINGO MODEL

The Shingo Model develops sustainable enterprise excellence through the application of Guiding Principles and a cultural system of continuous improvement that employs a variety of scientific tools and methodologies. The following figure (Chart 23.1) illustrates the major aspects of the Shingo Model and is available from the Shingo Institute website at www.shingo.org. The website and the Shingo Institute course series supply

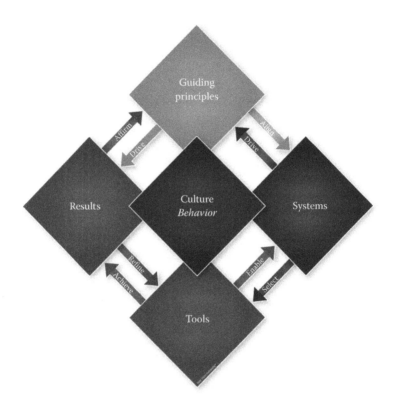

CHART 23.1
Shingo Model.

detailed support and explanation about each of the elements of the Shingo Model and the Guiding Principles.

The Shingo Model utilizes 10 Guiding Principles that will promote a culture of enterprise excellence. The following figure (Chart 23.2) illustrates the 10 Guiding Principles and is available from the Shingo Institute website at www.shingo.org. A detailed explanation of each of these Guiding Principles can be found in Chapter 7 of this book.

The Shingo Model also identified Three Insights of Enterprise Excellence which are available on their website at www.shingo.org/ and are quoted as follows:

INSIGHT #1 – IDEAL RESULTS REQUIRE IDEAL BEHAVIORS

Results are the aim of every organization, but there are various methods by which they are attained. Ideal results are those that are sustainable over the long term. Simple learning or buying new tools or systems does not achieve

CHART 23.2
Shingo Institute Guiding Principles.

ideal results. Great leaders understand the cause-and-effect relationship between results and behavior. To achieve ideal results, leaders must do the work of creating an environment where ideal behaviors are evident in every employee.

INSIGHT #2 – PURPOSE AND SYSTEMS DRIVE BEHAVIOR

It has long been understood that our beliefs have a profound effect on our behavior. What is often overlooked, however, is the equally profound effect that systems have on behavior. Most of the systems that guide the way people work in our companies were designed to create a specific business result without regard for the behavior that the system consequentially drives. Many systems are de-facto [sic] systems that have evolved in response to a specific need for a particular result. Managers have an enormous job, and this should be their primary job, to realign both management and work systems to drive the ideal behavior required to achieve ideal business results.

INSIGHT #3 – PRINCIPLES INFORM IDEAL BEHAVIORS

Principles are foundational rules and help us to see both the positive and negative consequence of our behaviors. This fact enables us to make more informed decisions, specifically, about how we choose to behave. The more deeply leaders, managers and associates understand the principles of operational excellence and the more perfectly systems are aligned to reinforce ideal behavior, the greater the probability of creating a sustainable culture of excellence where achieving ideal results is the norm rather than the aspiration. This is what the Shingo Model illustrates.

23.4 SUCCESS STORIES

There are many organizations that have experienced significant successes by applying a principled approach to Lean. One such company is Goodyear Tire & Rubber Company. Norbert Majerus has been the Lean Champion at Goodyear for over a decade and has successfully applied Lean tools to the R&D process in ways that originally were believed to be applicable only to manufacturing processes. Similar to the Shingo Model, Majerus used a principled approach to Lean in order to establish an understanding of the fundamentals of what Lean is, rather than simply understand how to use Lean tools. In his book, *Lean-Driven Innovation*, Majerus writes the following:

> Knowing the principles will let lean practitioners see opportunities in their company, their work, and the world around them. A lot of people confuse tools with principles. They learn tools and "randomly" apply them, often to the wrong problems and wonder why they did not work.

Majerus, 2017

A complete list of the Shingo Prize winners since 1988 is available at http://shingo.org/awards. It includes companies like Ball, Rexam, Goodyear, John Deere, Johnson and Johnson, and Abbott, as well as government agencies, and military establishments from countries all around the world. The Shingo Prize has been acclaimed as the "Nobel Prize for Enterprise Excellence."

23.5 SUMMARY

The Shingo Model creates sustainable enterprise excellence using a cultural approach that employs Guiding Principles, a system of continuous improvement, and effective improvement tools. The cultural approach to enterprise excellence established by the Shingo Institute produces ideal results by focusing on encouraging ideal behaviors. This approach to continuous improvement bridges the gap between improvement tools and sustainable enterprise excellence.

> The most stupendous improvement plans in the world will be ineffective unless they are translated into practice. Often at this stage the resistance of habit will prevent shop workers from implementing improvement plans. Indeed, such plans cannot be fully realized unless consent is obtained along with understanding and unless tenacious efforts are sustained.
>
> *The Sayings of Shigeo Shingo*, p. 107

24

Breakthrough Thinking

24.1 INTRODUCTION

Breakthrough Thinking was developed by Gerald Nadler and Shozo Hibino and recorded in their book, *Breakthrough Thinking*, first published in 1990. Breakthrough Thinking is an innovative thinking paradigm that produces a creative approach to problem solving. Problem solvers typically employ techniques, methods, and tools that have worked in the past. The Breakthrough Thinking paradigm develops innovative solutions by focusing on an ideal future state. Rather than focusing on the past, it focuses on the future. If you're always looking back, you'll always be behind.

24.2 SEVEN PRINCIPLES

Breakthrough Thinking employs seven principles called "The Seven Principles of Creative Problem Solving." These seven principles work together to produce solutions that are creative, innovative, and effective. The seven principles are listed and explained in the following sections.

24.2.1 The Uniqueness Principle

We can't solve our problems with the same thinking we used when we created them.

Albert Einstein

The Uniqueness Principle establishes the fact that every problem is unique. No two are alike. In fact, how could they be? Considering the vast number of variables involved in problems, it would be virtually impossible to find any two problems that involve the exact same problem solvers, stakeholders, circumstances, environmental forces, juncture, schedule, etc.

> It is not difficult to demonstrate that no two problems can be alike. No matter how similar two situations may appear on the surface, they almost certainly differ in terms of time, place, people involved, related surrounding conditions, and purpose of solution.
>
> **Nadler and Hibino, 1994**

What's the benefit of recognizing every problem as unique? Simple. If every problem is unique, then every problem deserves a unique solution. That means that you can't use the same solution on a new problem that has been used in the past. When you treat each problem as unique and deserving of a unique solution, you can prevent the narrow-minded copy-cat approach to problem-solving that is created by habitually reusing the same solutions repeatedly. Truly innovative solutions can never be developed without a unique approach to problems.

> We should request situation-specific solutions, and not focus on generalized truths or facts. Conventional thinking focuses on generalization and similarity, whereas Breakthrough Thinking focuses on situation-specific solutions and uniqueness.
>
> **Plenert and Hibino, 1998**

24.2.2 The Purpose Principle

The Purpose Principle involves expanding your perspective of a problem to consider the hierarchy of purposes while deriving the problem's solution. In the Purpose Principle, we ask the question, "What is the purpose of solving this problem?" We do this twice, the second time asking, "What is the purpose of that purpose?" If, after the second question, we do not have a purpose that focuses on the Strategic Objectives of the enterprise, then we should quit working on this problem. Solving the problem would not gain us anything of value. Solving problems for the fun of solving problems is a waste.

The Purpose Principle involves understanding the pure essence of the problem and often involves multiple variations of the problem as it is redefined based on various perspectives. By examining the substance of the problem and redefining it as needed, more innovative and higher level creative solutions can be developed.

It is common for students of mathematics to get in the routine of familiarizing themselves with the mechanics of how to solve specific types of problems. They memorize the steps they need to take to solve the common problem types they expect to be confronted with on an upcoming exam. However, when they're faced with a problem involving the same mathematical subject, but requiring some variation of the typical steps to solve it, they become unable to develop a solution. Because they don't understand the purpose behind the steps, they are unable to adapt them to variations of the problem.

> Our current turbulent age calls for the pursuit of the essence of everything. We should ask what should be, or what is the ideal, or what is the purpose, rather than focusing on data and planning the future as an extension of the past. Traditional reductionist thinking is fact and data centric and is the basis of "truth," whereas in Breakthrough Thinking we adopt a systems philosophy focusing on a holistic systemic view, where "purpose" becomes the focus.
>
> **Hibino, Noguchi, and Plenert, 2018**

24.2.3 The Solution-After-Next Principle

The Solution-After-Next Principle requires that problem solvers keep one eye on the future as they work to solve problems in the present. It involves having a clear vision of the long-term mission and avoiding the short-sightedness that can often limit our approach to a problem. Solving problems with the ultimate mission in mind will help develop long-lasting solutions, instead of short-term quick fixes.

> Think and design futuristic solutions for the focus purpose and then work backward. Consider the solution you would have recommended if in 3 years you had to start all over. Make changes today based on what might be the solution of the future. Learn from the futuristic ideal solution for the focus purpose (pull thinking) and don't try learning form the past and present situation (push thinking).
>
> **Plenert and Hibino, 1998**

The Solution-After-Next Principle requires the foresight to be able to not only consider what it will take to solve the problem this time but also what can be done now to make solving the problem easier the next time it comes up. We've all worked in organizations where the same problems seem to continue to come up. Executing the Solution-After-Next Principle requires not only fixing the problem at that time but also considering what can be done to solve the problem in the future as well. If we must repeatedly fix the same problem, then we are following the Einstein philosophy, which defines insanity as follows: "continuing to do the same thing and expecting different results."

> The solution-after-next principle elevates your thinking beyond the obvious first solution. If you have machinery that isn't working well, an engineer can redesign a gear to make the machinery work better. But you should also ask yourself, can we improve the solution either by refining the gear mechanism to still further advantage, or even by finding an entirely different way to do the job?
>
> **Nadler and Hibino, 1994**

24.2.4 The Systems Principle

The Systems Principle requires the problem solver to consider how the employed solution will affect other aspects of the system. It requires a holistic approach to problem solving, rather than focus only on the immediate effects of the solution.

Anyone who's worked on a construction site no doubt has experienced the challenges of what can happen when a subcontractor completes his or her scope of work without any consideration for the next crew coming in after him or her. Imagine the issues that can arise when the framing crew takes no thought for the plumbers or electricians who will have to run lines through the framing once it's completed. Imagine the issues the finish carpenters will face if the drywall crew was sloppy with their corners instead of making them square and plumb. It is not uncommon for subcontractors or sub-consultants to solve one problem only to unknowingly create several more down the line.

24.2.5 The Limited Information Collection Principle

The Limited Information Collection Principle recommends problem solving based on selective data collection, rather than digging through large amounts of data that are more likely to obscure the solution rather than highlight it. It focuses on only collecting and analyzing the data essential for solving the problem. It is common for problem solvers to become so involved in collecting and analyzing large amounts of data pertaining to the problem, for example, in Six Sigma, that they are developing an excessively thorough knowledge of the problem. However, this principle stresses that we first study the problem using a GEMBA process and then, when we have a focus on the problem, we collect only the data specific to that problem. Contrary to what information technology teaches us, all data are not good data. The purpose of the data is not to become an expert in data collection, the purpose is to solve a problem. The data collection and analysis process should be focused on the data that strive towards a solution, rather than look at all aspects of data that surround the problem.

> It is a mystery why people continue to use the congenital approach of inundating themselves with data, facts, and information about the present status of a system or problem area when they start a project. Great quantities of human effort are squandered in learning "everything." People falsely assume that a problem can be solved by throwing data and statistics at it.
>
> **Nadler and Hibino, 1994**

24.2.6 The People Design Principle

The People Design Principle requires that the individuals who will be responsible for carrying out the solution be involved in the problem-solving process. Too often, a manager will develop solutions for staff members to carry out but will not involve the staff members in the problem-solving process. Typically, the ones who have the most intimate understanding of a problem are the staff members who have been dealing with it on a regular basis. They are the ones who would be most likely to develop a simple and effective long-term solution.

Additionally, solutions should be sufficiently flexible to allow staff members to apply them in the most reasonable way. Rigid solutions typically are only applicable to the immediate situation and may fall short of solving the problem as it occurs in situations that may be slightly different. Allowing some flexibility in the solution empowers employees to apply the solution in a way that makes sense for their situation. A customizable solution is a more user-friendly solution.

The People Design Principle has two primary benefits. The first benefit is that involving the individuals who will be responsible for executing the solution will give them ownership of the solutions.

No matter how wonderful an idea is, if the employees don't support it, it will die. No matter how poor an idea is, if the employees have ownership in the idea, it will succeed.

Plenert and Hibino, 1998

The second benefit of the People Design principle is that by involving more individuals in the process of developing a solution, a better solution is achieved.

Many ideas grow better when they are transplanted into another mind than the one from which they sprang. No one is as smart as all of us.

Nadler and Hibino, 1994

24.2.7 The Betterment Timeline Principle

The Betterment Timeline Principle focuses on developing solutions that have elements of continued improvement over time. Because change is constant, an effective solution must constantly improve. It is likely that today's solutions will become tomorrow's problems if they do not improve. This means that the principles of Breakthrough Thinking should be applied on a continual updated basis.

The Betterment Timeline Principle makes solutions effective for the future. The solutions regularly have to be changed and upgraded toward the solution-after-next target.

Plenert and Hibino, 1998

24.3 SUMMARY

Breakthrough Thinking is a forward-looking, innovative, and creative approach to problem solving. If your focus is on the future, you'll soon find yourself there. If your focus is on the past, that's where you'll remain. One of the most powerful aspects of Breakthrough Thinking is that it is not a simple problem-solving tool, but a problem-solving paradigm. It treats problem solving as an operational practice and, thus, creates an organization of continuous, innovative problem solving.

25

Leadership and Strategic Excellence

The first problem in what we call improvement is to get a grip on the status quo. The most magnificent improvement scheme in the world will be worthless if your perception of the current situation is in error.

The Sayings of Shigeo Shingo, p. 27

25.1 INTRODUCTION

The United States military has always been labeled as an authoritarian, top-down leadership style, and that label is appropriate when it comes to command decisions during a time of crisis or combat. However, all the military bases employ civilians, and in many of them, the number of civilians greatly outnumbers the active duty military who are on the base. One day, one of the authors of this book met with an Air Force General who stressed, "We have been making changes for years. We have been using Lean and Toyota Production System tools, and we get the occasional improvement, but I haven't seen any overall sustainable improvements. Are you going to do any better?"

The General's concerns were real. And these concerns connect directly with all the aspects discussed in this book, like a cultural shift, empowerment of employees, and strategic alignment. So, where is the solution? The steps towards improvement are not something that can be corrected with one quick fix. Transformation requires making the time commitment to achieve the necessary cultural shift. Let's consider one example. In the Air Force, when new parts are introduced from a new vendor, a first article inspection process is initiated. The intent of the first article process is to make sure that the new part will test out as successful under the stress of air flight.

The first article process was lengthy and time consuming, taking more than 6 months and sometimes requiring years. The parts backlog included hundreds of products. This often causes planes to be grounded until replacement parts could be deemed flight worthy. An author of this book was asked to look at this process to see if the cycle times could be reduced. The author took on the challenge through a series of steps. He interviewed the leaders and workers involved in this process. Then, he organized a Rapid Improvement Event (RIE), requiring both the leadership and the employees to participate. Having the leadership there caused employees to be hesitant to share their concerns, but their presence demonstrated the level of commitment needed to show employees that the need for improvement came from the highest levels.

Employees were concerned. They asked questions like: "Fixing this is going to take money. We're going to need to move walls and add equipment. Where is this money going to come from?"

Leadership was quick to assure them that the funding would be available and that the directive to make the changes is coming from the highest levels of the Air Force. With that assurance, the employees felt empowered to make recommendations, which included a reorganization of the layout of the facility. Walls were moved, doors were cut out, and equipment was installed.

The employees felt a new level of freedom. When they saw that their recommendations were being approved and implemented, they felt empowered to make even more changes, this time to the software tools that they were using. After about 1 year of making changes and implementing new systems, the average cycle time for parts going through the system was measured in weeks. And the backlog of new parts was now measured in single digits and was down to only a few parts. The success for all of this is credited to employee empowerment because of a leadership commitment trusting the ability of their employees to make a difference. And it was credited to leadership showing employees that there was a strategic focus.

A critical element of managing strategy and establishing continuous improvement is effective leadership. The leadership of the organization must develop and maintain a focus on a clear vision and maintain the support of the organization in a united effort to realizing that vision. The leadership team must be the ultimate evangelists for the strategy of the organization and should work to maintain a focus on the realization of objectives. The organization's strategy begins and ends with the organization's leadership. If the employees do not believe the leadership team is committed to the strategy, they will be unlikely to take it seriously, as described in the following excerpt:

> Strategy without leadership goes nowhere; leadership without strategy has nowhere to go.
>
> **C. L. Harshman**

25.2 CHARACTERISTICS OF AN EFFECTIVE LEADER

Leadership is a very broad topic and countless books have been written on the subject. Here we will not attempt to explain all the many aspects of effective leadership, but rather we will list a few of the characteristics of an effective leader that have the greatest impact on an organization and continuous improvement.

25.2.1 Empowers Others

Empowering others begins with trust. A leader that empowers others is one who is both trusted and trusting. A leader who is not trusted by those he or she is attempting to empower will fail due to a lack of confidence. Employees must know they can trust your opinion, your values, your character, and your motives if they are to feel empowered by your leadership. The empowering leader will take responsibility for the team's failures and pass on credit for the successes to the team that made them happen.

A leader must not only be trusted but also trusting to be able to empower others. Leaders, especially leaders who are also technical experts in their fields, tend to want to control operations to the point that every job is executed in the way they would do it themselves. Empowering others requires trusting the expertise of those you have working for you. Trust them to do the job, provide them with the necessary training, mentoring and support, and they will often surprise you how well they're able to fulfill their responsibilities. The employees that you empower will become so good at their jobs that they'll become better at them than even you. Controlling your employees will only hold them at your level, rather than inspiring them to rise above it. Review the story at the start of Chapter 12 where the

Leadership gave up control of the employees and realized that the only way they could improve is by empowering their employees. Also, review the story in Section 5 of Chapter 17 where leadership adjusted the compensation to transform their organization.

> A World Class Manager doesn't have to offend someone else or make someone else look small in order to make himself or herself look good. A World Class Manager looks good because he or she is good! World Class Managers build themselves by building others.
>
> **Plenert, 1995**

25.2.2 Always Learning

Truly innovative and effective leaders are constantly learning. They seek to learn from books, observation, research, engaging with colleagues, etc. They see problems as opportunities to innovate and they see failures as valuable lessons. They possess an eagerness to expand their understanding and are constantly looking for something new to read or study. Learning, for a leader, is not an obligation, it's a passion.

> Leadership and learning are indispensable to each other.
>
> **John F. Kennedy**

25.2.3 Maintains a Clear Vision

It's hard to follow someone who doesn't know where he or she is going. Likewise, it's hard to convince others to follow you if you're just going in circles. Vision is the prerequisite for leadership. In the absence of vision, leadership becomes pointless. Maintaining a clear vision ensures that leaders can keep the big picture in mind and are not easily distracted by focusing on the little things. A clear vision keeps the organization moving in the right direction, establishes confidence, and eliminates hesitation and doubt.

> Good business leaders create a vision, articulate the vision, passionately own the vision, and relentlessly drive it to completion.
>
> **Jack Welch**

25.2.4 Lead from the Front

Employees respect and follow the leader who isn't afraid to get his or her hands dirty. A leader who leads from the front is one that is action oriented and focuses on being involved in the efforts of the organization, rather just dictating them. Active involvement builds unity and demonstrates the leader's commitment to the organization's mission and achievement of strategic objectives. Leaders who inspire action are those who lead from the front of the team, not from behind the desk.

> People ask the difference between a leader and a boss. The leader leads, and the boss drives.
>
> **Theodore Roosevelt**

25.2.5 Results

The true evidence of how effective and influential a leader is, is the unity and effectiveness of the organization. If an organization is failing to achieve success and the leader is placing blame on the employees or looking for who to fire, then the leader should resign. The failure of an organization is always due to a failure in leadership. Poor leadership is the most common cause of unhappy employees and unhealthy workplace cultures.

A great leadership team can turn around a failing organization and develop it into a successful enterprise that employees can be excited to be a part of. The fastest way to turn around any organization is to turn around its leadership, as expressed in the following:

> An army of sheep led by a lion can defeat an army of lions led by a sheep.
>
> **African Proverb**

25.3 SUMMARY

A common misconception about leadership is that a title or position is what makes an individual a leader. What makes you a leader is not your position but your influence. Additionally, the leaders of an organization are not only located at the top floor in the corner offices. They exist throughout the organization and at all levels. They can be found pushing a broom on the construction site, sitting in a small cubicle crunching numbers, and sitting in the boardroom. When the top-level leaders use their influence to empower the organization, leadership becomes a shared responsibility.

> It is impossible to improve any process until it is standardized. If the process is shifting from here to there then any improvement will just be one more variation that is occasionally used and mostly ignored. One must standardize the process before improvements can be made.
>
> **Masaaki Imai**

26

Conclusion

Are you too busy for improvement? Frequently, I am rebuffed by people who say they are too busy and have no time for such activities. I make it a point to respond by telling people, look, you'll stop being busy either when you die or when the company goes bankrupt.

Shigeo Shingo

26.1 STRATEGIC EXCELLENCE

The author was brought in on a project for a high-tech company in Seattle, Washington. This company had been selling a product for 10 years with a great deal of success, so much so that they didn't worry about sales. The markup was big enough to cover any costs. But now, they were receiving some stiff competition. They were no longer experiencing the position of being the run-away sales leader in the gaming equipment. They had to become more competitive. Margins were tight, and forecasts of which products would sell were often wrong. They decided that they needed to revise their strategy to one that was more customer based and that addressed competitive elements. Their strategy had to shift from one where they told the market what they were going to get, into one where they listened to the market and paid more attention to what the customer wanted.

A large team was assembled to address the new marketing challenges. The team included stakeholders from a variety of elements of the organization, including some advanced technologies. They recognized the challenge that 80% of their sales occurred in a 6-week period right before

Christmas. If forecasts were wrong, they would produce the wrong products, and they would end up with a large amount of obsolete inventory and, of course, lose their window for sales.

The team identified several problem areas, including that fact that a lot of their lost sales were the result of stock-outs of products that were in demand. When customers went to purchase the product, and it wasn't available, they would resort to a competitor's product. In the end, the changes that needed to be incorporated included both a better understanding of customers' expectations and a redesign of the forecasting and materials management systems.

This story stresses several messages:

1. A strategy that is not focused on the customer's expectations will end up opening the door for competitors
2. A strategy which doesn't focus on products and services being available for the customer will open the door for competitors
3. A system that hasn't been designed to support the needs of the customer is a waste
4. Forecasts should be based on leading indicators based on the customer's expectations, rather than on lagging indicators based on past sales

Don't wait until your competition is beating you down to the ground before you review your strategy. Strategies that are not reviewed regularly and that don't focus on the principles of the enterprise are worthless. A strategy needs to be the lifeblood of the organization. If it isn't, then your organization becomes a random, unmanaged accident.

Throughout this book, we have laid out the step-by-step process of planning and managing an organizational strategy. Through the strategic planning process, we've discussed how to examine current internal and external conditions in the Analyze Phase and how to clearly outline the strategic plan in the Define Phase. Through the strategic management process, we've discussed how to effectively implement the strategy and align the organization in the Execute Phase and how to solve problems and promote continuous improvement in the Refine Phase. Numerous techniques and methods have been discussed throughout each phase that will accelerate your organization beyond the typical strategic planning process and on to the level of Strategic Excellence.

At this point, it should be very clear that Strategic Excellence cannot be achieved without a healthy and vibrant organizational culture. An organization lacking in a healthy culture will never accept full ownership of even the most elegant strategic plan. Additionally, a vibrant culture cannot be achieved without an inspiring vision supported by a clear plan of action and obvious momentum. Strategic Excellence and a vibrant culture are a synergistic partnership in the sense that their combined effect will unquestionably produce far more than they could ever produce independently, as aptly described:

> Rather than merely telling people to work better, it is much more productive to set out clear objectives and to provide motivation.
>
> *The Sayings of Shigeo Shingo,* p. 6

26.2 FINAL THOUGHTS

Strategic planning and management can be a daunting task, but when you have a clear understanding of how to go about it, it should also be very exciting. The Strategic Excellence approach can create exciting improvements in performance, behaviors, client satisfaction, and cultural vitality. By applying Strategic Excellence, you and your organization will be able to find opportunities for improvements throughout your organization. As you take advantage of opportunities to improve your organization, you will move into a position that will make your competitors irrelevant. Even if your competitors try to copy some of the things you do, they will never be able to copy who you are. That's the essence of what makes Strategic Excellence such a powerful approach. It's not just about deciding what the organization will do, it's about deciding what the organization will be. And, as Toyota has been known to declare, "They can copy us all they want. By the time they catch up with what we are doing today, we will have advanced by several years and will still be ahead of them."

As you look at your organization, you may feel that the process presented in this book is something that should have been initiated years ago. It may be true that the best time to start this process may have been some time ago. But the second-best time to start it is right now. Get excited for Strategic Excellence, you're now ready to make it your reality.

If we want to achieve improvement we must first have the mental flexibility to believe that even though there is only one summit, there are many paths we can tread to reach it. If we adamantly think that the current methods are the best and no other means are possible, improvement ideas will never emerge.

Kaizen and the Art of Creative Thinking, p. 85

References

BOOKS

Barr, S. (2014). *Practical performance measurement: using the PuMP blueprint for fast, easy and engaging KPIs*. Samford: The PuMP Press.

Chermack, T. J. (2011). *Scenario planning in organizations: how to create, use, and assess scenarios*. San Francisco: Berrett-Koehler.

Hibino, S., Noguchi, K., & Plenert, G. J. (2018). *Toyota's global marketing strategy innovation through breakthrough thinking and kaizen*. Boca Raton, FL: CRC Press.

Kaplan, R. S., & Norton, D. P. (2006). *Alignment: using the balanced scorecard to create corporate synergies*. Boston, MA: Harvard Business School Press.

Kim, W. C., & Mauborgne, R. (2016). *Blue ocean strategy: how to create uncontested market space and make the competition irrelevant*. Boston, MA: Harvard Bus Review Press.

Liker, J. K. (2004). *The Toyota way: 14 management principles from the world's greatest manufacturer*. New York: McGraw-Hill.

Majerus, N. (2017). *Lean-driven innovation: powering product development at the Goodyear Tire & Rubber Company*. Boca Raton, FL: CRC Press.

Martin, K. (2012). *The outstanding organization: generate business results by eliminating chaos and building the foundation for everyday excellence*. New York: McGraw-Hill.

Maxwell, J. C. (2005). *Developing the leaders around you*. Nashville, TN: Nelson Business.

Nadler, G., & Hibino, S. (1994). *Breakthrough thinking*. Rocklin, CA: Prima.

Plenert, G. J. (1995). *World class manager: Olympic quality performance in the new global economy*. Rocklin, CA: Prima Pub.

Plenert, G. J. (2012). *Strategic continuous process improvement: which quality tools to use, and when to use them*. New York: McGraw-Hill.

Plenert, G. J. (2018). *Discover excellence: an overview of the Shingo model and its principles*. Boca Raton, FL: CRC Press.

Plenert, G. J., & Cluley, T. (2012). *Driving strategy to execution using lean six sigma: a framework for creating high performance organizations*. Boca Raton, FL: CRC Press.

Plenert, G. J., & Hibino, S. (1998). *Making innovation happen: concept management through integration*. Boca Raton, FL: St. Lucie Press.

Shingō, S. (1987). *The sayings of Shigeo Shingo: key strategies for plant improvement*. Cambridge, MA: Productivity Press.

Shingo, S. (2011). *Kaizen and the art of creative thinking: the scientific thinking mechanism*. Bellingham, WA: Enna Products Corporation.

WEBSITES

The Shingo Institute at Utah State University. (n.d.). Shingo Institute. Retrieved September 15, 2017, from www.shingoprize.org/.

Strategy Execution Thought Leader. (n.d.). Retrieved September 24, 2017, from https://jeroen-de-flander.com/.

Index

A

A3 problem solving, 149, 152, 180, 182
Action items and goals, 117
Action plan, 119–121, 125
Actual cost vs. projected cost, 99
Actual revenue vs. projected revenue, 98
Agile/agility, 1, 31, 60, 68, 79
Air Force, 213–214
Albert Einstein, 155, 167, 183, 207
Alvin Toffler, 87
Always learning, 216
Analysis approach, 16
Analyze phase, 11
Approach to define, 61
Approach to refine, 174
Assure quality at the source, 69

B

Backlog volume, 96
Bad behaviors, 94–95, 113
Balanced scorecard, 149–152
Blue Ocean Strategy, 81
Bottleneck analysis, 188–190
Break-even point, 97
Breakthrough thinking, 17, 134,
    207–212
Building engagement, 5, 111, 153
Buy-in
    build, 91, 128, 129
    enterprise-wide, 110, 129
    enhance, 60–61, 166
    organization-wide, 5, 111
    strengthen, 61

C

C.S. Lewis, 66
Cascade/cascading
    process, 140
    strategic objectives, 122

throughout the organization, 141, 159
    vs. fragmenting, 137–142
Cause-and-effect analysis, 182
Challenging current process, 104
Characteristics of a good metric, 108
Characteristics of effective leadership, 215
Characteristics of effective
        communications, 166
Characteristics of effective goals, 118
Characteristics of good governance, 144
Characteristics of good objectives, 85
Chermack, T., 19
Clear direction, 60, 138
Client acquisition cost, 99
Client lifetime value, 98
Client onboarding, 162
Client relationship, 16, 36, 41–42, 143
Client relationship analysis, 41
Client satisfaction, 97
Collaboration, 103
Commercial performance analysis, 36
Communication, 165
Competitive advantage, 14, 47, 174
Core competencies, 16, 74–74, 83, 127
Cost, 99
Create constancy of purpose, 69
Create value for the customer, 70
Creating too much work, 106
Cultural analysis, 29
Cultural approach, 7, 196, 200, 204
Cultural shift, 126, 200, 213
Cultural transformation, 156
Cultural vitality, 221
Customer focus, 106
Customer-based perspective, 80

D

Dashboard report, 151
Dave Crenshaw, 142
Deep dive, 151

For Product Safety Concerns and Information please contact our EU
representative GPSR@taylorandfrancis.com
Taylor & Francis Verlag GmbH, Kaufingerstraße 24, 80331 München, Germany

www.ingramcontent.com/pod-product-compliance
Ingram Content Group UK Ltd.
Pitfield, Milton Keynes, MK11 3LW, UK
UKHW021830240425
457818UK00006B/143